GETTING IT RIGHT

Laurie Graham

GETTING ◀●IT●▶ RIGHT

A Survival Guide to Modern Manners

Cartoons by Gray Jolliffe

Chatto & Windus
LONDON

Published in 1989 by
Chatto & Windus Ltd
30 Bedford Square
London WC1B 3SG

A CIP catalogue record for this book is available
from the British Library

ISBN 0 7011 3452 6

Photoset by Rowland Phototypesetting Ltd
Bury St Edmunds, Suffolk
Printed in Great Britain by
Mackays of Chatham plc, Chatham, Kent

*This book is dedicated to my mother, who still
makes me write thank-you letters on December 27th.*

CONTENTS

SIX EASY WAYS TO OFFEND

Be constantly aware of your own importance.

Light a cigarette.

Keep a dog.

Take a bottle . . . drink it all yourself.

Roar with laughter *before* swallowing the guacamole and tortilla chips.

Dress for the bedroom, then go out for lunch.

. . . AND SIX STEPS TO NICENESS

See a gaffe, cover it.

See a gaffe that can't be covered, ignore it.

Answer invitations.

Say thank you, properly.

Give up telling the story of your life.

Never assume *anything* about *anyone* you just met.

INTRODUCTION

Etiquette is dead. Long live manners!

Etiquette labelled us. Above all it was the method used by Old Money to distinguish itself from New Money and No Money. A funny thing this. Old Money was itself once New Money, and before that it was No Money, Just a Few Old Flints. Old Money accumulated what it has by pillage, plunder and marriage – pretty strong stuff compared with dealing in scrap metal or playing the futures markets, but there we are. Old Money doesn't always like to be reminded that mankind came into the world empty-handed and must leave it the same way, even when it owns half of Scotland.

The point of **etiquette** was always to fix our class origins. Or our aspirations. People who wished to appear more elevated in society than their birth would strictly allow, lost sleep over a thousand complicated rules. Is this the way gentry would eat an orange, or ask for the lavatory? Or is asking for the lavatory a thing true gentry never do?

The sad thing about etiquette is that you can never get the better of it. Being inquisitive about it labels you, being anxious about it excludes you. Of course it does. That's why it was invented. Either you know and care how to address a duchess or you do not. There can be no halfway house with a duchess, unless her own good manners are greater than the sum of etiquette, protocol and snobbery.

The point of **good manners** is to make *everyone* feel accepted and at ease. The truly well-mannered have little interest in etiquette, although they may be familiar and confident with every detail and every pitfall. Etiquette is as likely to hinder good manners as to encourage them.

Manners are common sense. Etiquette is full of artifice.

People who are obliged to spend the larger part of each day in the company of others have difficulty in maintaining such qualities as compassion, forbearance, and blind eyes. Is it any wonder? Good manners require a perfect marriage of selflessness and self-interest. A willingness always to think, 'What is this person suffering? How may I make them feel better? And is there anything in this for me?'

Manners are the art of considering a situation from everyone's point of view, including one's own. Society used to help in this by erecting barriers against unwelcome intrusion. There were servants. And no telephones. Just imagine how much easier it must have been to be civil in the days of calling cards, letters and pistols at dawn. Modern barriers are not nearly so elegant. Lies aren't very stylish. Answering machines even less so. But we all need to draw a line somewhere.

Is honesty the best policy? Not in polite society. Honest is what you can be with those who know you very well. Sometimes it's a good way to start with people you hope to know very well. But there is hardly any place for it at sherry parties. If you like sherry parties and look forward to being invited to many more, white lies, sublety, and evasion will do you a lot more good.

When someone asks me 'Laurie, tell me truly, no punches pulled, can I wear lime, and what do you think of Mervyn?' what I am most inclined to do is open a bottle. Pushed harder, 'No, go on, I'd give anything to know whether you think I suit a dropped waistline,' I will oblige, but only because a readiness to oblige is even more essential to good manners than benevolent insincerity.

Sincerity is a dangerous commodity. I don't want to know

what anyone really thinks of me. You don't want to know what
anyone really thinks of you. It would be too painful. Trust me.
What's more, it doesn't matter. We are all less than we would
like to be. Good manners forbids us from painting in the details.

I hear the footsteps of the Moral Majority heading my way.
Manners are nothing to do with morality either. Except for this;
morals often put their owners on the spot. It is for the well-
mannered to help them stay there. If that's where they want to
be. 'I'm afraid I make it a rule never to gossip about the
indiscretions of my married friends,' remarks a bundle of fun in

a hair shirt. The normal human response to this is 'Yes, I'd heard Phyllis was putting it about a bit. But do you think there's anything in the flagellation story?' and the well-mannered ask 'Cream and sugar?'

The best place to be horrible is at home. This hardly needs saying. Most of us do it quite naturally. When fireside manners slip out in public, the consequences can be desperate. What passes for reasonable use and abuse within the family is often very embarrassing for bystanders. Or very funny. That can be even worse. Anyone with a reputation for being a bit of a wit and a wag is in constant danger of temptation. The temptation to fill the public wash-house, two shows nightly, and get a laugh a minute out of the dirty linen. Funny people can be very bad-mannered. Unfortunately, the converse is not true.

Of course the world is full of reasons for bad manners. About sixty billion at the last count. Some are worse cases than others. Some are without hope. If you have an urge to improve people, here is a new furrow for you to plough. With the aid of this book you will be able to redirect the uncouth on the use of fish knives. Sadly, when you are done, the world will not be a better place. That requires imagination, foresight, and inner calm.

Many of us now live in circumstances which deter good manners. Anyone living or working in a large city has to contend with unwelcome noise, smell, and physical contact. Clearly etiquette has nothing to contribute. Centuries of accumulated lore that was once relevant to people who rode horses, carried swords and walked in fear of slop pails from above, will do little to sweeten interpersonal relations on the Northern line at rush hour. But manners might.

Certain members of the Royal Family and aristocracy have exquisite manners. They achieve this through hard work and long solitary trudges across grouse moors. If the Balmoral

Effect is not available to you, use the art of manners to create distance or reduce it.

Manners clarify, deflect, alleviate and enable. If you wish merely to get the better of an artichoke, turn immediately to page 88. For manners, be so good as to read on.

HI! I'M JEN

Excuse my asking, but whatever happened to introductions? Those of us who came of age in the Sixties or later know of them only by hearsay. We were the 'Sling your coat there and grab a beer' generation, and somehow, when we were all young and revolting it didn't matter. I mean, like wow man! Who cared about names!

I'm afraid a lot of us have never lost those hang-loose habits. We like to show exactly how laid back we are about serving drinks to the chairman and his wife by saying, 'Come in! Mind the cat! Greg, Mo, Trish, Penny, George, Angus, meet Bernard and Mrs Bernard, sorry, I didn't quite catch . . . Anyway, there's Bellini in the jugs, Bulgarian Red or fizzy water, so do pitch in. It's every man for himself.' What this actually demonstrates is how we are too unsure of ourselves to introduce people properly. We would rather be bad-mannered, but call it relaxed.

In the end this catches up with you. You get a little older and go to parties without any of the following thoughts:

a **I wonder whether I'll get laid?**
b **I wonder whether I'll get high?**
c **Should I take a bottle?**

You go to stand around in little clusters and murmur. Often it's not a lot of fun, and it's especially not a lot of fun if you don't know who you're murmuring to. You may have been told, cursorily, 'Laurie, meet Mbmbmbm. Nick for the third time of asking will you open another frigging bottle!' But an introduction like that forces you to make a cold start all by yourself.

Whoever Mbmbmbm is I'd love to meet him. Truly. Where shall I begin? How about, 'May I introduce myself. I'm Laurie Graham, and I'm an usherette on the afternoon shift at the Leigh-on-Sea Odeon. I'm sorry I didn't catch your name.'

There! Wasn't that easy! There is now a small chance that old Mbmbmbm will remember me for five minutes. With a bit of help from our hostess not only might he have remembered me, I might have remembered him, and we should have had something to murmur about. What a tragedy that introductions are no longer cool.

The following conventions are very old-fashioned and very useful. Once you have remembered them and used them a few times you'll discover how much better they make everyone feel. They are long-winded by modern standards. They slow down the pace of events, and for that reason if no other, they are to be recommended.

- The young are always presented to those older, the less distinguished to the greater, and when all else fails, male is presented to female. If you include crowned heads in your guest list you are supposed to reverse the usual male to female rule, but then, if you entertain royalty I expect you already know that.

- It is sufficient to say each person's name once, provided you say it clearly. 'Larry? Harry! Harry? Larry!' sounds very silly doesn't it?

- Elderly people are not always happy to be introduced by their first names. They take the view that there will be time enough for that if the relationship develops. They're quite right.

- Man to man, **handshaking** is still the thing. Women have a little more choice but not much. A woman need never feel obliged to be the first to offer her hand. But if a hand is offered her it is, needless to say, the worst possible manners to refuse it. Even if it's not a very nice hand.

  The main thing about handshaking is to decide what you're going to do and do it. Doing the Hokey-Cokey with your right hand is all very well at Christmas parties, but not when you are being introduced to an Air Vice-Marshal. Dickering around is bad manners. Dickering around even *sounds* like bad manners.

8

- **The correct response to an introduction is:** 'How do you do?' Polite society will not accept 'Charmed, I'm sure', 'Pleasedtermeetcha' or 'Your place or mine?'

- Introducing one person to fifteen others who are already on their second glass is a fool's errand. Far better to introduce the newcomer *properly* to one or two conveniently placed people and then let society take its course.

- In public, think before you introduce anyone. In your own house, guests accept being introduced to new people as one of the hazards of your friendship. They know that one of the prices they must pay for dinner is to be introduced, and they either trust your choice of guests or refuse your invitation. But in public there's no saying who you might be lumbering with whom

    When chance circumstances bring together two people you know who will not necessarily be keen to know each other, a few words and a speedy exit are the safest course. For example, if I knew Frank Sinatra and I ran across him whilst out with my Aunty Vi, I would not introduce them for fear of Aunty Vi embarrassing us with a request for Frank to sing 'My Way' right there in the Kilburn High Road. See what I mean?

    The best thing is to say, 'Frank! How lovely! Aunty and I are in a tearing hurry to catch the Co-op before closing time, but do let's get together soon.' Then go. Even if you have to carry Aunty Vi kicking and screaming all the way.

- Clarity is everything. Usually. Taking your time to say, 'Gloria, I'd like you to meet Archie, who's just back from the Golan Heights,' covers the ground beautifully. Gloria and

Archie now know each other's names *and* have something to talk about.

But there are occasions when **the conversation piece** should be very carefully selected. This is especially true of people in certain professions. I don't know any doctors who like to have their profession revealed by an introduction. I have a friend who is a Doctor but not a doctor who hates to be introduced as anything but Jack the Scientist because people do have a tendency to start stripping off for a free medical examination right there amongst the empty bottles. Lawyers will tell you similar stories. Also dentists, who get shown bridgework by people who have just eaten three sausage rolls.

- Sometimes, the less said the better. I'm often asked, 'Laurie, what is the currently accepted procedure when introducing my son's gay lover to Great Uncle Herbert?' This is easily answered. You just say, 'Herbert, I'd like you to meet Randolph. He's a young friend of Stephen and he has the most fabulous collection of fishing flies.' No need to embellish.

   If Great Uncle Herbert has seen anything of life and is sufficiently interested in Stephen and Randolph to give their relationship a second thought, he may draw his own conclusions. And if Randolph feels like throwing a Coming Out party it will be up to him how he handles it. But I would no more feel the need to explain Stephen and Randolph's private lives than I would to say, 'Shirley, do meet Nigel. Nigel likes to do it covered in olive oil and tied to the bed.'

- And so to **couples**. In some circles it is still done to introduce people as Mr and Mrs Bertie Heckmondwyke. Some women wouldn't feel right introduced as anything else. Personally, if

I'd married Bertie I'd still like to be introduced as Laurie. You will know which of your friends feel the same way.

Worse than being introduced as Mrs Bertie, is being introduced as Mrs Bertie whose husband is something terribly interesting in insurance. I think that's very bad manners. If you are a Mrs Bertie and this is ever done to you, try using this tart but effective rejoinder: 'How do you do. My name is Vera and I'm pretty interesting myself, actually.' This is not very well mannered, but you'll feel so much better after you've done it that you will be divine company for the rest of the evening.

My award for **Introduction of the Year** goes to a lad, young enough to be my own son, who recently fought his way across a crowded marquee calling, **'Laurie! There you are you dreadful old tart! I want to introduce you to Louise who is most definitely not my wife.'** As introductions go this was vulgar, disrespectful, and irregular. But it reduced three hundred people to fascinated silence and it ensured that none of us will ever forget Louise.

And what if you're not Mrs Bertie at all, but people will keep assuming? There is a lesson for us all here. First, don't assume, ever. Second, avoid excruciating labels. Live-in lover, popsie, sugar daddy, co-mortgagee, are all things to think but not say. We all have names. We should use them.

'Camilla, I'd like you to meet Willie Whalley and Dot Scott.' You could go on to say, 'Willie and Dot live together with her five children and his mother in Cheadle,' but why bother? The closeness of their relationship only matters if Camilla takes a fancy to Willie. Or Dot. If she does, it would be very bad-mannered to try and do anything about it so soon after meeting, and there will be time enough for everyone to make clear where their loyalties lie.

And if Camilla assumes? If it really matters to you, tell her. But it would be better manners to let her mistake pass, *unless* you expect to have a lot to do with Camilla in the near future. If that's the case, a small embarrassment now is better than a bigger embarrassment later. Keep the tone light:

'Oh Willie's not my *husband*! We're just paying off the same mortgage!'

PRESENTING

Never introduce yourself to **Royalty**. If you find yourself being presented to the Queen, or the Queen Mother, you should call her *Your Majesty* the first time you speak and *Ma'am* (pronounced *marm*) thereafter. Similarly, Princes and Princesses and Royal Dukes and Duchesses should be addressed as Your Royal Highness and then as Ma'am or Sir. That said, you aren't likely to end up in the Tower if you use Ma'am or Sir throughout.

You don't introduce Royalty to anyone. You *present* commoners to Royalty. You just say, 'May I present Nora Cudlipp.'

Dukes and Duchesses who aren't Royals can be treated differently. If you need to address them, call them *Your Grace*. Dukes and Duchesses rank so high in the social pecking order you are unlikely ever to need to introduce them to anyone. Just in case, you say, 'Sir, may I present the Duke of Duckworth.' In the more likely event of introducing someone of lower rank to the Duke, you should say, 'May I introduce Nora Cudlipp,' and by way of explanation to Nora, 'The Duke of Duckworth.'

A Dowager Duchess usually gets abbreviated to Duchess in these circumstances, and a divorced Duchess should be referred to as Doreen, Duchess of Duckworth, because there may be another Duchess of Duckworth flashing her new wedding ring around the same banqueting suite.

Marquesses, Marchionesses, Earls, Countesses, Viscounts and Viscountesses, Life and Hereditary Peers, and all associated dowagers and divorcees can be introduced as *Lord* and *Lady* followed by the surname, and addressed as *Your Lordship* or *Your Ladyship*. It is not necessary though to stick *Your Lordship* into every sentence you utter.

Baronets and Knights and their wives should be introduced as *Sir Dickie and Lady Duckworth*, and referred to in the same way in conversation.

A Dame should be introduced as *Dame Nora Cudlipp* and afterwards referred to as *Dame Nora*.

If you meet an **Ambassador**, call him *Ambassador*.

If you meet a **high-ranking clergyman** call him *Archbishop* or *Your Grace, Cardinal* or *Your Eminence, Bishop* or *Your Lordship, Mr Archdeacon, Mr Dean*, and, when all else fails, *Sir*.

Anyone else should be addressed by their private rank.

So, if you have the bad luck to find yourself in charge of a Marchioness, a Bishop, and your husband's Uncle Ted who was Mayor five years ago, your script should run something like this: 'Lady Potterton-Boiler, may I introduce the Bishop of Milton Keynes, and Ted Biggins.' Pause. And then to Uncle Ted and the Bishop, 'The Marchioness of Potterton-Boiler.'

If the worst happens and your mind goes completely blank, say, 'Could I please leave you to introduce yourselves? I'm afraid Peregrine just ate the gerbil.' Then eavesdrop. That's important. If you don't eavesdrop you'll never find out who your guests are.

LIP SERVICE

Social kissing has arrived. It didn't have to wait for the Channel Tunnel to open. A nation that resisted horse-meat, tasteless apples and Napoleon has accepted the most Gallic of customs without a whimper. Nowadays few ask themselves 'Do we?' The question today is: 'One cheek or two?'

Some people have always kissed. In my youth unnecessary kissing suggested theatrical leanings, or a flaw in the Anglo-Saxon pedigree. When my father's relations came visiting from Rio de Janeiro, the neighbours were put straight about the kissing. 'They've been too long in a hot climate,' we explained. 'There was never any of that when they lived in Leicester.' That was the 1950s. Gestures of welcome and farewell were then seen in three very distinct forms. They labelled your class origins, loud and clear.

The toiling masses greeted you with 'Hrrmph', muttered from behind *The Sunday Pictorial*. The middle classes worried about shaking hands, seeming too chummy, telling you where the toilet was and whether they should have called it the toilet. Gentry used the elegant choreography of the self-confident. They rose to their feet, shook hands, and when appropriate, pecked you lightly and dryly and withdrew. We can learn from them.

TO PECK OR BE PECKED

The decision to kiss is yours. The decision to be kissed is not. No matter how whiskery or slobbery you expect the imminently arriving kiss to be, it is unpardonably ill-mannered to refuse it. You have no need to return it. But when you see those lips heading your way you must offer a cheek.

Whatever your sex, if you decide to make the first move, it is your lips you offer, not your cheek. The difference between the two gestures is small but important. Offer your cheek to someone who's busy trying to get their arm down the sleeve of their

overcoat, and you are likely to be left standing, head cocked, and alone.

Some kisses are difficult to effect. A big difference in heights, or an armful of parcels will be an obstacle. And if both of you have been worrying for half an hour over whether you have a strictly handshaking relationship or can safely move on to warmer gestures, the forecast isn't good. Most likely you'll end up pumping hands and banging noses all at the same time.

A kiss on the hand is chancy. It used to be a rather theatrical but respectable public gesture but it is now so rarely seen, that it is embarrassing to receive. It reeks of the chaise-longue. It makes you suspect that the perpetrator has been asleep for a hundred years, or is very drunk indeed. And it makes you realise how badly your cuticles need doing.

Garlic and designer stubble apart, worry is the greatest enemy of the social kiss. If being a kisser bugs you, confine yourself to receiving kisses graciously. Even from someone with breath like a constipated Bulldog. And if you feel really comfortable with kissing, never forget the rules:

- Lips and cheeks only.
- Keep your powder dry.
- Brevity is everything.
- In the event of a heavy cold, mislaid dentures, herpes, or retained bubble gum, revert to the warm handshake.

NAME-DROPPING

As if life isn't hard enough, there are names waiting to catch you out. Surnames which sound different from the way they look. There is something intrinsically bad-mannered about these names. The world is divided into those who know how to pronounce them and those who do not. And those who do not know wish they did, whatever else they may say.

The following list is not exhaustive, but you should consider yourself very unlucky if you ever run into more than five or six of these names in a whole lifetime.

ALNWICK	is pronounced	*ANNICK*
ALTHORP	„	*AWLTRUP*
BETHUNE	„	*BEETON*
BROUGHAM	„	*BROOM*
BUCCLEUCH	„	*BUCKLOO*
BURGH	„	*BURRA*
but BURGHLEY	„	*BERLY*
CHOLMONDELEY	„	*CHUMLEY*
COLQUHOUN	„	*KERHOON*
COKE	„	*COOK*
CECIL	„	*SISSIL*
DALZIEL	„	*DEE-EL*
DEVEREUX	„	*DEVEROOKS*
DOUGLAS-HOME	„	*DOUGLAS-HUME*
FEATHERSTONEHAUGH		*At least three possible ways. Ask.*
HERVEY	„	*HARVY*
HAREWOOD	„	*HARWOOD*

KNOLLYS	„	NOLES
LEVESON GOWER	„	LOOSON GORE
MAINWARING	„	MANNERING
MARJORIBANKS	„	MARCHBANKS
MENZIES	„	MINGIES. But not always.
MILNES	„	MILLS
PONTEFRACT	„	POMFRET
RUTHVEN	„	RIVVEN
ST JOHN	„	SINJUN
STRACHAN	„	STRAWN
THYNNE	„	THIN
VILLIERS	„	VILLERS
WEMYSS	„	WEEMS

THE COMPLEAT LETTER WRITER

So few letters get written these days, even in the course of business, that to receive one at all is cause for celebration. Almost no one cares any more whether you've used a lined pad from Woolworth, or something engraved with your address. Red paper, yellow paper, scratch 'n' sniff paper, it doesn't matter. If it has a beginning, a middle and an end, and all three can be deciphered, you're onto a winner.

Nor does it matter if you prefer to type. If your handwriting is poor, typewritten letters may be a relief to all concerned. Only the sender of a deeply personal letter can judge whether typing will set the wrong tone. A letter to the bereaved or sick will *seem* more sincere if it is handwritten, but the bereaved and the sick would rather receive something typed on the inner bag of a cornflake packet than nothing at all.

Personally, I love letters. This is just as well because I get a lot of them, many of them from total strangers. They always begin by apologising for taking up my time, but there's really no need. The only letter I ever wished I hadn't received was one that came without a signature or the courtesy of an address for a reply, full of justifiable complaint about my ignorance of correct grammar. Anonymous letters are appalling manners.

If you worry about Good Form you cannot do better than to write with a fountain pen on a nice big sheet of plain paper, sign it legibly and stick it in an envelope, folded as little as possible.

No one worth bothering about is going to say, 'My dear! Did I tell you those dreadful people from Burgess Hill invited us for a weekend? Of course we shan't go. The letter was written in ballpoint!'

HOW TO BEGIN

Dear Dickie is fine. *My Dear Dickie* is warmer. And *Sweetest Dickiepoohs* is a private matter between you and your Platignum.

Dear Dickie Duckworth is a beginning that I find rather awkward, but it does have its uses. Such as when writing to someone with a damn fool unisex name like Laurie. Or Ned. I replied to a letter from a Ned recently. *Dear Mr O'Reilly* I wrote. A few weeks later we met. She was very nice about it, and rightly pointed out that anyone else would have jumped to the same conclusion, but I still felt a perfect fool.

AND HOW TO FINISH

The only thing wrong with *Yours Sincerely* is that people can't remember how to spell it. When in doubt, *Kind Regards, Best Wishes* and *Yours* are all acceptable alternatives in roughly ascending order of warmth.

The addressing of envelopes is a subject that never fails to bring the sticklers out of the woodwork. Strictly, one should use Mr D. Duckworth or Dickie Duckworth, Esq., and for his wife, Mrs Dickie Duckworth. This distinguishes her from his ex-wife, Mrs Olive Duckworth, and his widowed mother, whom some might address as Mrs Hattie Duckworth, others as Mrs Dickie Duckworth Senior.

In practice, the use of esquire can be consigned to the same dustbin as collarstuds and spats. And many women feel as uncomfortable as I do being addressed as the old man's spare tyre. I never address any woman, no matter how devotedly and idyllically married, as Mrs Dickie Duckworth. I use her very own given name, and risk being dropped by Quality Folk.

GONGS

The question of letters after names only arises when you are writing to strangers. There are three categories to consider. Big Gongs. Minor Gongs. Gongs for Valour.

By Big Gongs I mean Orders of Knighthood, or Companions of Honour. Sir Dickie Duckworth, KBE, will do. If Sir Dickie has a string of honours, it will still be enough to put the two most important ones after his name.

OBEs, MBEs and CBEs are what I mean by Minor Gongs. If your letter is formal and you're sure which honour applies, put it in – Dickie Duckworth, OBE.

Many people decorated for bravery prefer to keep quiet about it. If you're writing to someone who is in the Armed Forces, give him his decorations. Otherwise leave it.

TITLES

There is no escaping the fact that a lot of people with titles do care about being correctly addressed, and that even when they couldn't care less, those of us untutored in these affairs lose sleep over getting it wrong.

Getting it Right
Letters to **Royalty, and Dukes and Duchesses**, can safely be started *Sir* or *Madam* – though, if you're a stickler for etiquette you should address the Duke as *My Lord Duke* – and concluded *I have the honour to be your most humble and obedient servant.*

Apparently one can drop the word *humble* for a Duke or Duchess without causing great offence.

Letters to **Marquesses, Earls, Viscounts, Barons** should begin *My Lord*, if the tone is formal – but again, *Sir* will get you by – and their wives should be addressed as *Madam*. But if you're inviting them round for beans on toast, *Dear Lady Foxhunter* will do. You should end with *Yours Faithfully* or *Yours Sincerely*, depending on the reasons for the letter and the warmth of your relationship.

An **Hon.** is a Mr, Mrs or Miss and you can write to them as such. Just remember to put *The Hon.* on the envelope, and don't attribute rank where none is due. If The Hon. Persephone Foxhunter marries plain old Dickie Duckworth, a letter to the happy couple should be addressed to Dickie Duckworth and the Hon. Mrs Duckworth.

Ambassadors are Excellencies. Their partners are not. An envelope should therefore be addressed to His Excellency the Austrian Ambassador and Frau Lederhosen. When in doubt, if you absolutely must have the Turks in and you don't know the Turkish for Mrs, phone the Embassy and ask. Or call her Mrs. She won't mind. To conclude a formal letter to an ambassador you must become a humble servant again. More informally *Yours Sincerely* will do.

An **Archbishop** is *Your Grace*, a Bishop may be *My Lord Bishop* or *Dear Bishop* depending on the tenor of the letter. An Archdeacon is a Venerable, but being full of Christian humility he will find *Dear Mr Archdeacon* an acceptable alternative to *Venerable Sir*.

High Court Judges are knighted on appointment if they are not already peers. For some reason this throws people into disarray.

'What is your answer?'

23

'I don't really know, Your Eminence.'
'Come now! I wish to hear your reply.'
'Well, Your Celestial Magnificence . . .'
'Yes, yes! Speak up!'
'I'm sorry Your Effulgent Luminosity, I've forgotten the question.'
'For Chrissakes, Angela, I only asked you if you'd marry me!'

Relax. Out of court you can address a judge like any other mortal. With a knighthood. *Dear Sir Neville*, you start. Sir Neville and Lady Quartersessions, you write on the envelope. Of course, if you get done for fraud and Sir Neville tries your case, you'll be back to calling him *My Lord*.

Magistrates are different. In court a magistrate is Your Worship, and envelopes containing official business should bear the letters J P after the surname. Privately there is no need to refer to the matter at all. To send a Christmas card addressed to Mr and Mrs Beaky Chesterton J P is a nonsense.

Similarly, with **Mayor**, who is officially *Your Worship* or *Mr Mayor* whatever his gender. If he is a stranger to you, or you are writing on civic business, give him his due, and remain *Your Worship's obedient servant*. If you've known Kath and Lionel since they were both in Junior School, write *Dear Kath and Lionel . . .*

AND FINALLY

Letters of Reference or Introduction, which are more often a burden than a pleasure. A letter of reference should be honest, obliquely if not directly. Any prospective employer who fails to read between the lines of a lukewarm reference deserves what he gets. It is also permissible to refuse a reference if it is not in your heart to give it. It is a courageous thing to do, but not bad-mannered. If you are handing a reference to the person it concerns it should be in an unsealed envelope.

Letters of introduction to be presented by the introducee are not much used now it's so easy to phone New Zealand and say, 'A girl called Poppy from Pinner might contact you. Could you be a sweetie and show her a good time while she's in Auckland? Just one thing though. Don't let her anywhere near a sherry bottle.'

This is rather a shame, because a telephone call, especially a quick one to New Zealand, doesn't give the recipient time to think. A much better way is to send a letter, telling New Zealand *exactly* what it is you're lumbering them with, and timed so that it gets there before Poppy does. Isn't that what you'd prefer if you had to change places? And isn't putting yourself in someone else's shoes what good manners are all about?

And if you find yourself on the receiving end? If your sister writes and asks you to be nice to Louis from Fort Lauderdale? Or Louis from Fort Lauderdale turns up on your doorstep with a letter from your sister? Remember this:

- The British have an international reputation for mean and begrudging hospitality to strangers.
- They deserve it.
- Louis from Fort Lauderdale may be a schmuck. He may be a very special person you wouldn't have missed for anything. Only one way to find out.
- Afterwards you can always write to your sister:
  Dear Sis, Louis showed up as promised. He drank all my Scotch, blocked the drain, and ran off with Maureen. By the way, I've given your address to Loathsome Leslie from Letchworth. He'll be in Florida next month so I told him to be sure to look you up.

Use your best joined-up writing, address the envelope clearly, using the zip code, and be sure it is adequately stamped. That way no one can have any grounds for complaint.

GUESS WHO?

The telephone is such a useful invention. You can dial Australia and tell someone who's feeling sad that you love them. You can order a pizza. And you can be very bad-mannered without anyone seeing you. Bad-mannered because you can baffle or inconvenience people without them being able to do a thing about it. Nearly everyone who does it, does it because they have no imagination. They have never given a thought to what it's like to receive one of their calls.

When you dial a number the safest assumption to make is that the person who picks up the phone at the other end doesn't know who you are or what you want. Tell her. Don't begin with:

'I'm ever so sorry to bother you but Susan said you wouldn't mind her giving me your number . . .' or: 'You don't know me but . . .'

And *never* say: 'Guess who?'

Just say: **'This is Peggy. I'd like your advice on chain saws,'** or: **'This is Peggy. I've phoned you for a long moan about Albert.'**

And always add **'Is this a good time for us to talk?'** You may just have cleared your desk, made a pot of coffee and lit a fag, but the person you're calling may be neck deep in something.

Calling someone at work to talk to them socially should be your last resort. Even on a very slack day it is embarrassing to have to respond to 'Can you pick up six Chicken Kievs, the dry cleaning and my Birth Pills, and what did I hear you saying to your mother about Boxing Day?' and excruciating to deal with 'Do you love me? I really miss you. Tell me you really miss me.

What's wrong. You don't love me any more, do you? Tell me you love me or I'll put my head in the microwave,' with all of Grants and Loans Section C eavesdropping.

If the person you were calling isn't available the wisest thing always is to say you'll call back. Holding is money and time wasted. Messages too often fall down the back of a radiator. If you must leave a message, the pithier it is the better your chances of its getting passed on accurately. And don't leave a string of numbers where you might be reached at different hours of the day. Leave the number that is the best bet, and hope.

Increasingly the likelihood is you'll get an **answering machine**. For the sake of you and your phone bill I pray it isn't one with a message designed by a wag. Answering machines have brought the comedians out in force. And the impersonators of interesting accents. I don't know about you, but I don't want to hear my cousin Bernie banging on in a defective Charles Aznavour about how sorry, how really sorry he is not to be around to take my call, and all at my expense.

Do you remember Jim Rockford? He had a machine long before Bernie did. 'This is Jim Rockford,' it said. 'Leave your name and number after the tone and I'll get right back to you.' Perfect. Get out your pencil and add this to your list of Things To Do – **Prune my answering machine message in the style of Jim Rockford.**

And if you get a machine and have the patience to hang on till the end of the message? Use it, why not? If you're phobic about them you're not alone. But the more you do things you fear, the smaller the fear gets, and machines are a much safer way of getting a message to Cousin Bernie than leaving it with the cleaning lady or Aunty Vera.

Just say who you are, what you want, and for a truly efficient finish say what day it is and what time. Then, when Bernie gets back from Denmark two weeks later he'll be able to work out that he's missed seeing you in the audience on *Question Time*.

When your telephone rings the most sensible thing to do is to say your name or your number. Growling into the mouthpiece doesn't tell anyone anything, except perhaps that the person who answered the phone is in a foul mood. It's a very bad-mannered thing to do. I do it. Nearly everyone I know does it. Basically we're all nice people who hardly ever get out of the wrong side of the bed, but you'd never guess it to hear us answering our phones. I would promise to try harder, but the

unidentifiable growl does have its uses. It opens up the possibility of dodging the unwanted call.

Call-dodging sounds like bad manners. But wait. Some calls are unsolicited time-wasters. Everyone with their number in the directory gets pestered sometimes. And everyone gets calls that they are not quite ready to receive. Years ago I discovered that my customary 'Hm?' when I answered the telephone sounded nothing like me in full flood. I was mistaken for my husband, and for the lady who did the ironing. I've only ever used this to say, 'She's not in,' but it has saved me from many conversations

I wasn't in the mood for. And think of the possibilities! With enough nerve you could say, 'Naah, he's in the Falklands for six months. I'm just feeding the fish,' and be rid of someone forever. Well . . . for six months at any rate.

And if the call is from someone you do want to talk to, but they are sluggish starters? Allow them their **warm-up time**. When they ask, tell them how you are. Ask them how they are. Then say, 'So how can I help you?' Keep the conversation going with little murmurs of encouragement and don't let it wander too far off the beaten track. If Mrs Taylor calls to see whether you can do one hundred bridge rolls for the Whist Drive and gets bogged down in Timothy's GCSE grades, guide her back on course. Say, 'And what exactly do you want me to do?'

Then, go for **a strong finish**. People will love you for it. After fear of making calls, the next commonest fear is not being able to end a call. Having said their piece and unburdened themselves of Timothy and the Whist Drive, they let their concentration slip. They spiral downwards into the price of margarine, the best caravan site in Bude, and a synopsis of last night's episode of *The Archers*.

Be a brave person and put them out of their misery. Say, 'That will be fine, Mrs Taylor. Thanks for putting me in the picture. Goodbye.' A bit terse? Not really. Those three sentences sum it all up, and said with warmth they will never offend. In fact people will say, 'She may be useless at filling bridge rolls, but she's got lovely manners.'

CONVERSATION PIECES

The world is full of little people who fear no one is interested in them. Sadly they are nearly right. We hurry through life full of our own thoughts. Occasionally we stop to think, 'Conversation? Count me out! I'm shy,' or, 'Conversation? Certainly. Why don't you all sit back and relax while I play this record entitled *My Life and Incredibly Fascinating Times*?'

This is no help to anyone. Everyone needs to say things. Everyone needs to hear things. Making it happen, oiling the wheels of small talk, is the backbone of good manners.

Small talk is not really the same thing as conversation, but it may bring you nearer to it. Engaged in small talk, you are feeling your way. In the long run it may lead to more exciting things. Most likely it won't, but as you never can tell you shouldn't try and skip it. Even if you are a thousand times busier than everyone else you meet, even if the world is full of ignorant fools and you are God's gift to quantum mechanics, you should hop down off your pedestal and do your bit. It's a very reasonable price to pay for being part of humanity.

WHAT TO DO IF YOU'RE SHY

Stop it at once. Shy is boring. **Shy is bad-mannered.** Shy is also universal but no one who takes refuge in shyness will ever believe that. Typically, a shrinking violet is convinced that everyone they meet has been tipped off in advance. 'Laurie?

Not *Laurie the Mogadon Cocktail* Laurie? Don't tell me *she's* going to be there! You poor thing!'

See how self-important shrinking violets can be?

Whatever you perceive your social handicap to be – the wrong school, the wrong religion, the wrong bri-nylon cardigan – spare a passing thought for those lion-hearted people who go to parties in spite of *real* problems – stammerers, lipreaders and involuntary twitchers, foreigners who don't have the language, and all those who have been disgraced or dumped publicly, and in glorious Technicolor.

Now get up off your dignified tush and make someone's day. **Be the first to speak.**

BUT WHAT SHALL I SAY?

Say, 'Hello, I'm Denzil Parrott. Have you tried some of this wonderful stuff with red peppers?' This may light the blue touchpaper of chit-chat.

'Leonard Fretwell,' he may respond, 'I never eat peppers myself, but the salted almonds are very good. Are you in Sewage too?' And away you go.

On the other hand, Leonard may not be such a pushover. He may look at your plate anxiously and say, 'No.' Don't be downhearted. Coax him.

Say, 'I can't imagine life without red peppers. What do you like to eat?' You now have Leonard Fretwell by the conversational short and curlies. He can't get away with 'Yes' or 'No.' You have used the ultimate weapon, **the Open Question**.

OPEN QUESTIONS

Open questions begin with words like *Why*, *Where*, *What* and *Who*. They force people to formulate answers that contain statements of fact or hope and invariably give rise to more questions. They act like a fertiliser on sterile ground. An open question may sound more inquisitive than a dead-ender – compare 'Do you come here often?' with 'How often do you come here?' – but it always pays dividends.

If you find talking to strangers difficult, examine your usual conversational gambits. **Avoid dead-enders.** Pursue the Why and the Wherefore of people. Before you know where you are you'll be talking Sewage with Leonard Fretwell.

SEWAGE AND THINGS

Some subjects are pretty certain to be safe ground. Food is one. Even hyper-allergic vegans have to eat. Travel is another. Those nearest and dearest to you may never want to hear another word about Viareggio but Leonard may be fascinated.

If you're not good at small talk, think of some safe but interesting subjects and practise at home. Practise on your children if the grown-ups won't play. They will add this to the accumulating evidence that you are a brick short of a load, but tell them they'll thank you some day. Some day when they've had to get through a six-course dinner partnered by the President of Murmansk Chamber of Commerce. It is one of the most useful ways you can prepare children for adult life.

The golden rule of conversational foreplay is this: Never assume anything. Sexuality, politics, religion, sense of humour . . . take them gently or not at all. When you ask something, listen to the answer. Listen to what is said. Above all, listen to what is not said. Don't tell jokes. Don't call people *fascist* or *pinko*. And don't gossip. Oh, go on then. But be careful.

Reckless bitching obeys Sod's Law of Coincidence. This law states that in a gathering of eighty people the one to whom you confide that the old lady in the portrait hanging over the crab vol au vents is quite the ugliest old lady you ever saw, will turn out to be her nearest and most affectionate living descendant.

VERY IMPORTANT PEOPLE

Wheedling Leonard out of his shell may not be an enjoyable experience, but you have the advantage of being in the driving seat. How much worse to be saddled with a Treasury Minister or the greatest existential philosopher in Gwent? You probably don't know anything abut the Euro-dollar. And even less about Kierkegaard. It doesn't matter. At least, it shouldn't matter.

Experts need light relief. A Treasury Minister may be deeply grateful to you for your tips on growing tomatoes. Don't be afraid to add the common touch. The people who will like you for it will heavily outnumber those who thin; you unspeakably trivial.

Being Very Important is a state that exists mainly in the eye of the beholder. Senior statesmen and Great Thinkers are set apart from the rest of us by just one talent or one piece of good fortune. We have more in common with them than not. Irrational fears, consuming vanities. The truly great never forget this. That's why they are ready and very willing to talk to *anyone* and to make them feel, however briefly, that there is no one in the world they would rather be with.

Many Very Important People don't know this, so you are now a step ahead of them. Next time you think you are about to be overwhelmed, when you can see that Nigel is about to introduce you to Sir Peter Puffadder who is certain to have you marked as an insignificant little oik, stop, and remember that Sir Peter has his weaknesses. Also his vices. Instead of smarting from his snub, amuse yourself by imagining what they might be. And then move on.

MOVING ON

Some conversations have no natural end. This is especially true at parties where you do want to talk to people, but not to the same three people all evening.

If you are in a group, make your excuses and detach yourself decisively. If you are lumbered, one to one with someone dreadful, the procedure is harder but you should still do it. It would be rude to hog Leonard Fretwell all evening. Here is the technique:

You decide to move on. You prepare Leonard for this by perceptibly increasing the physical distance between you as you talk. You then give Leonard the opportunity to move on with you to another group. Say, 'Let me introduce you to Betty and Albert, they're *such* interesting people.' If Leonard falls in with your plan you can then judge for yourself the right moment to move on again, leaving Betty and Albert to cope

Yes, I did need rescuing but there was no need to say it in front of her

in their own way. If there isn't a Betty and Albert conveniently to hand, say firmly, 'Please excuse me. I have to make a phone call/move my car/find the bathroom.' Then go.

And don't come back for ten minutes. It may take Leonard that long to ensnare someone else and you owe him that opportunity. You don't owe him anything else.

TEN THINGS BEST LEFT UNSAID

Have you heard the one about St Peter and the Rabbi?

When's the baby due?

Of course, all Arabs/Eskimos/Men/Social Democrats . . . are the same.

What does your husband do?

Don't I recognise you from the clinic?

When are you two going to get married?

Bill, you old bugger! Who was the crumpet I saw you with last night?

. . . The surgeon said he'd never seen one like it. To this day Frank doesn't realise how near he came to losing me. Anyway, I had thirty transfusions and six thousand stitches and I was back at the mangle within a fortnight. Everybody says what a marvel I am . . .

I'm in Rubber, for my sins!

I always felt *I* might write a book.

HOW TO BE A HEAVENLY HOST

The role of host carries with it great scope for demolishing stuffy old manners and inventing sensible new ones. A host has it in his gift to make people feel loved, cosseted and contented, or plain jittery, according to his inclinations and talents.

Being **a good host requires foresight, clarity, and imagination.** It is simple, but like many simple things, it isn't easily achieved. The bad news for guests is that it's a skill best learned on the job. For those who spend approximately the same proportion of time being a guest as they do being a host, this is acceptable. Pamela's pheasant may have been served a little too *saignant*, and her spaniel may have urinated on your Jasper Conran trousers, but as you recall only too well it was Pamela who managed without toilet paper in your bathroom, and wasn't it also Pamela who forgave you for serving the *salade aux feuilles d'automne* on the same plate as the insect course.

Some people are more often guest than host. Some people are absolutely never host. If it's because they are too mean or too lazy, eventually their phone will stop ringing. If it is because they are wonderful at being guests and like to stick at what they do best, they will never be short of somewhere to go. Better to be a gifted and glowing guest, than a host with clenched teeth and white knuckles.

A good host makes clear from the start what is being offered, what is not being offered, and what is expected in return. The invitation is your best opportunity to get all that settled in a straightforward way. As in:

Dinner, Friday 13th, 8 for 8.30, in the kitchen so no need for diamonds. Please let me know.

Or, more formally:

Boozy Hunt

Biffo and Cecily Neville
A T H O M E
Wednesday March 15th

RSVP   *Drinks, 6–8*
The Hangar
Snettisham

Biffo and Cecily have used an At Home card. Originally these cards weren't used as invitations at all, but as notices of intent. If Cecily had been around in the days when society ladies held court on certain afternoons, she would have used an At Home card to announce when she was willing to receive callers. If you dropped in at any other time you were likely to be told that Cecily was not At Home, even though she was sitting in the drawing room feeling bored brainless. The At Home card was used to keep droppers-in under control and I for one would welcome their return.

The form of the card has remained the same, except for the addition of RSVP. An invitation like this leaves Boozy in no doubt. It says *Drinks* so he shouldn't expect dinner. It says *6 till 8*, so he shouldn't loiter round the gin bottle until midnight. And it says *RSVP*, so he should. Otherwise Cecily may think he's not coming and decide to shampoo the carpets instead. Except she won't. Hosts whose manners are better than those of their guests always give the benefit of the doubt to people who don't reply. In a moment of bravado Cecily may say, 'Just let that jerk show up. I'll pretend we're not in.' But come 5.30 on the 15th she'll be polishing glasses and listening for the familiar sound of Boozy's Sunbeam Alpine.

Beware the telephone invitation. It is true that the telephone allows spontaneity between friends. But it allows very little manoeuvring room to those who wish to decline, and it is too easily mis-remembered and overlooked.

The same goes for invitations shouted across the street as I found to my own cost very recently. 'Sunday fortnight, drinks and food, can you make it?' called a friend. 'Love to,' I said. 'I'll put it in my diary immediately.'

Of course I didn't. First I finished polishing the door knocker, then the phone rang and well, what with one thing and another I never wrote it down. As Sunday approached I felt less and less confident about my memory. Had I counted the weekends right? Could she have said Saturday and not Sunday? And why was I being such a dithering fool? Why didn't I just call her up and say, 'Are you expecting us tomorrow?' I don't really know. I suppose it didn't seem like a cool thing to do.

Sunday came. I sent the Old Feller out on reconnaissance.

'Walk past looking normal and see whether the kitchen is a hive of activity,' I instructed him.

He reported back. 'Nope,' he said.

'What, no cupboards being gutted for glasses that aren't chipped? No Magimix turning out chick-pea dip? No one running around in pantyhose and a damp towel?'

'Nope.'

In other words there was absolutely nothing to suggest a party might be about to happen. We were on the point of taking off our glad rags and settling down with the papers. Then we saw the caterer's van drive past.

Wonderful party. If I'd had a little card with it all written down, I'd have looked forward to it even more.

INVITATIONS

How to make people feel loved, wanted and full of expectation *and* be certain you won't be left in the lurch with ten gallons of mulled wine:

- If you use the telephone *always* confirm at a later date, either by card that says To Confirm or by a purposeful phone call that includes the words 'I *am* looking forward to seeing you tomorrow!'
- If you are inviting a large number of people, cards are the easiest option. It doesn't matter whether they are engraved, printed, or written in blood on eighteenth century vellum. Just make sure your guests know exactly what you intend.
- There is a trend towards Regrets Only instead of RSVP, but I really can't see it catching on in a big way. I'm sure most hosts are like me – neurotic, obsessive, and, in spite of a 100% acceptance, utterly convinced that no one will show.
- Better than invitation cards, if numbers don't make it impractical, are letters. I'm a sucker for a letter myself.

> *Dear Laurie,*
> *As we've got an unspeakable amount of Beaujolais Nouveau to shift, and Norm's father is staying with us and he loves telling you about El Alamein, why not come to dinner Saturday week?*
> *Yours,*
> *Beryl*

Who could resist?

Beryl's letter is not a masterpiece, mind you. She doesn't make clear whether the Old Feller is also invited, though I'm sure he is. And she doesn't say what time. But that's because it's Beryl. She knows I'll phone her and say, 'Of course we'll come! Is it posh frocks? And am I supposed to know about the bankruptcy hearing?'

EYE OF NEWT AND TOE OF FROG

Mixing people is the toughest part of any host's job. When your courage fails, you can call in caterers. When you're feeling flat and uninspired, you can hire jugglers and a dance band. But only you can decide whether Gary Glitter and the Moderator of the Church of Scotland should break bread together at your table.

Here are some points that may help:

- Some people talk. Some listen. Few are blessed with both gifts in equal proportions. Around a table an approximate balance between the two works best.
- Away from the table, less stage-management is necessary. At parties guests can usually circulate themselves out of boredom or bother. Having said that, there are people who don't deserve to be anyone's guest. You may feel that you owe hospitality to someone who graduated from the Attila the Hun School of Charm. But don't you owe a collectively greater debt to your other guests? Don't you invite people principally so that they can enjoy themselves?

Someone asked me recently, 'How much time should elapse after a divorce before I can safely invite both exes to the same party?' Holding firmly to the pleasure principle my answer had to be 'A lifetime wouldn't be nearly long enough.'

- **Matchmaking** of any sort requires the lightest touch. Of romantic matchmaking I would say only one thing. Don't. Ignore me and you will have Sandra on the phone the next morning yelling, 'Is *that* what you call gorgeous?' You have been warned.
- **Engineering potential friendships or business deals** is scarcely less dodgy. You need to be very discreet, and alert. If things backfire you must be willing to abort the mission no matter what effort it has cost you to get your pawns into position. And you must know when to sit on your hands. There are people who do it as a career. Are you sure your Whitsun Fork Brunch is the moment to play Henry Kissinger?
- Then, can duty and pleasure be mixed? And what about **entertaining to impress**? Isn't that one of the most ill-mannered concepts of all time? Entertaining to make people feel special and wonderful – Yes. Entertaining to rub some-one's nose in your Chinese carpets, Waterford crystal, and ability to shell out for a butler – No.

Impressing is one of those things that everyone wants to do but no one wants to have done to them. Not even globe-trotting tycoons. *Especially* not globe-trotting tycoons. During my eighteen years as *châtelaine* I have done my share of duty enter-taining. The Old Feller's meteoric crawl up the career ladder is due in no small part to my Coq au Vin and rapier wit.

To be honest I have never met a business guest who hankered for puréed celeriac or lamb cutlets with little white hats on. None of them has ever darkened my kitchen doorway to say, 'Terrific! I haven't had Truffled Sausages with Coulis de Framboise in days!'

The thing your business guest would most like is to go home. He'd like to be sitting in his own little bit of real estate, eating potato crisps and drinking beer. The well-mannered host never forgets that. The further your guests have travelled the more cosseting they require. Even very big cheeses indeed long to take off their tie or unhook their panty girdle and eat ham and eggs. Unless they're Jewish. Or Muslim. Or Vegetarian.

GOOD MANNERS SHOULD MAKE DIETICIANS OF US ALL

First, when in doubt, ask. Second, the world is full of things that are good to eat. The fact that you are a legend in Penge for your Beef Wellington and your visiting luminary is a Hindu, is no reason to hit the Valium. The number of people with dietary restrictions is on the increase. Whether they are religious, medical, ethical or whimsical is unimportant. Once you have been made aware of them you must respect them. Whacking out a slice of cardboard pizza to a lone vegetarian while the rest of you eat Roast Duck will not do. Nor will making a big deal out of the lengths you've had to go to cook lentils. Big deals are bad manners.

You have been offered a challenge, so take it. There are few human beings who cannot satisfy their hunger satisfactorily with a meal composed of vegetables and fruit. You can revert to your own true preferences when Mr Dasgupta has gone home to Delhi.

GUEST CONTROL

Guests who do not know you well are best handled like small children – firmly but kindly. If you want them to come through for dinner, tell them so. Then tell them where to sit. I can never bring myself to write place cards. They don't seem quite *à propos* in a household where plastic dog turds make unsolicited appearances. But people really do need some guidance. Try to combine bossiness with charm:

'Winnie, sit there and don't move. I want you to take charge of this bottle while I deal with George and find us something to eat.'

If you want them to leave the table, stand up and tell them, 'We'll have coffee by the fire.' Tell them where the bathroom is. Bathrooms are no guessing matter. Strangle at birth all talk of helping with the washing up. Say, 'I have a little treasure who does them in the morning. He'd be furious if we touched his dish mop.'

The best way of dealing with late arrivals is to proceed without them. It's bad enough having a flat tyre in a blizzard on the M11 without the additional burden of knowing that seven people are eating too many nuts and drinking too much gin while Caroline's *entrecôtes bordelaises* are evolving into leather.

Late lingerers are a different thing. A well-mannered host has no control over them at all. Some people have the ability to keep going. Some people don't have to get up in the morning.

As a host I have sometimes fallen asleep on the job. It was very bad-mannered of me but the lingerers seemed not to notice so I suppose it didn't really matter. The best thing to do is to regard guests who don't want to go home as a perverse compliment. You would need only one experience of guests stampeding for the door after a single drink to prove this point.

OVERNIGHTERS

Before you ask anyone to sleep in your spare room, sleep in it yourself. This advice is often given and rarely taken.

Most people's spare sleeping arrangements are very spare indeed. And an uncomfortable bed may be the least of its

47

shortcomings. What about ice on the *inside* of the window panes? Or dogs which lie with their bottoms on the pillows? What about nowhere to hang anything, nothing to read, and the bedside lamp which delivers a high-voltage kick and no illumination whatsoever?

What does an overnight guest need?

He needs somewhere to be comfortable and private. You don't want him under your feet all the time and he doesn't want to be there. He wants to know the score concerning hot water, food and the personal quirks of any children or animals he might meet on the stairs.

He doesn't want to be walled up till eleven on a Sunday morning, dying for a cup of tea and a poached egg, while you sleep in, throw plates or screw heartily.

Provide him with the means of making a hot drink. If Trust House Forte can manage that, you certainly can. If you're very slow starters in the morning, put a tin of biscuits in his room as well. And if you absolutely do not have a spare kettle and have to take his tea to him on a tray, always knock and leave it *outside* his door. Yes, even if he's in there on his own. It may be your house but for the time being that room is his territory.

And if it's your house it's your lavatory. Guests do not want to have to complete three weeks of intensive study and practice before being able to flush your lavatory. Get a plumber in. Think of it as one small step towards being a heavenly host.

EVERYTHING TO PLAN

If you are in charge of the kind of dinner where the positioning of guests really does matter, the rules are simple. The foundation stones of a correct seating plan are that the most important woman sits on the host's right, and the most important man on the hostess's right. You then alternate the sexes until you run out of people.

Thus, if the fabulously influential Sir Dickie and Lady Duckworth are dining with you, and you've also invited Connie and Cyril from next door, your table plan will read

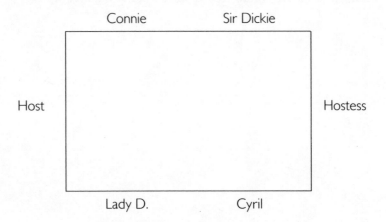

and the only question that then remains to be answered is, are Connie and Cyril really going to give you the right mix?

If you get ambitious and also invite that nice couple from

Saffron Walden, you've really got problems: eight people don't make for a nice symmetrical pattern. Try it.

Do you have time to go out and buy a round table? Round tables solve everything.

On the other hand, if you're stuck with an oblong table you can make a sensitive guest feel important by putting him or her at the end facing the host.

Suppose you have to seat a testy Sir Dickie, Lady Duckworth, and six other mere mortals including yourself and your partner. Put Sir Dickie at one end with the hostess on his right and the host facing him at the other end. Lady Duckworth sits on the host's right and everyone else fits in nicely.

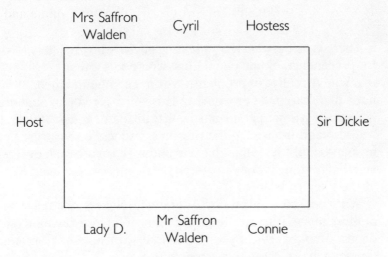

If your guests are the Dragon Empress of Tonbridge Wells and five also-rans, the solution is as follows: Empress at one end, with the host on her right, hostess at the other end with the Empress's partner on her right.

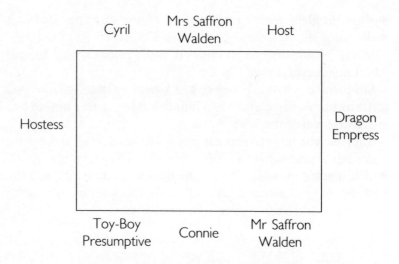

Cyril Mrs Saffron Walden Host

Hostess

Dragon Empress

Toy-Boy Presumptive Connie Mr Saffron Walden

There is no easy answer to seating guests who are likely to vie for precedence. Some people just won't be soothed.

If you've really got problems, why not compound them? Why not add a spare man or woman? This will force you to abandon all hope of symmetry and make you think more imaginatively. It will also add interest to the tiresome business of ensuring that husbands and wives don't have to endure each other all evening and that nothing is done to offend the dignity of ex-Queen Beryl of the Pitcairn Islands.

With foreigners, even slightly grand foreigners, the safest and politest course is to give them the seats of honour. I would only depart from that rule if your guest list also includes major, and I do mean major, home-grown nobility.

Let's look at the black side. Suppose you have to seat a Viscount, a Cardinal, and your brother-in-law who is a Rear-Admiral, newly out of the closet and courageously partnered by his boyfriend. There are three ways to tackle this:

- Consult *Debrett's*.
- Be decisive. Axe your brother-in-law. There's a time and a place for most things but this is not it. If the Cardinal is a foreigner make him Top Dog. There won't be a Mrs Cardinal, so the Viscount and Viscountess can share second and third prizes, according to the balance of power within their marriage and which of them you are most eager to impress. If they've heard about the Rear-Admiral you're probably onto a loser anyway.
- Tell them the table leg fell off so it's everyone down to the *Hoo Flung Dung* for a Vietnamese takeaway.

ON BEING A DIVINE GUEST

A good guest is a rare animal. He understands the nuances of punctuality, he recognises the difference between enough of a good thing and too much, and he knows how to say thank you and goodbye. If one of these people swims into your social pool, cherish him.

If you are a less than gorgeous guest, if you arrive drunk, pick fights and leave unconscious, isn't it time you did something about it? Even if your transgressions are small, wouldn't the world be a better place if you did as you would wish to be done by?

LESSON ONE

Being a good guest starts very early in the transaction. Invitations require a response. A host who says, 'We've having a few people in on Thursday. Do come if you're free,' is allowing you all the room she can to accept or decline. If she has made the same allowance to all her invitees she could end up not knowing whether to expect twenty, or none. No matter how casual an invitation, it should be carefully considered and answered. Better to say, 'I shall probably be out of town until late. If I'm back before ten would you still like me to turn up?' than to say nothing at all.

Always parry a word of mouth invitation you have any doubts about. It's kinder and wiser to say, 'Can I call you tomorrow when I've checked my diary?' than to say, 'Great! Love to!' and then put the phone down and think, 'Shit!'

Refusals that are less than genuine must be thoroughly researched. Someone, possibly someone very nice but very dreary, has taken the trouble to offer you hospitality. Good manners now require that you let them down lightly but firmly.

Don't say, 'Sorry, we'll be racing at Newmarket' when they might just realise there's no racing at Newmarket in December. Don't say, 'Dennis's mother's coming for tea,' when they know she lives in Vancouver. Tell them something utterly plausible that cannot be challenged. The ten minutes it will take you to work out your alibi is time well spent. Done properly it will let you off the hook and satisfy the host that you are declining with regret. Not *too* much regret though. If you lay it on too thick she may reschedule the party to fit your busy programme!

Acceptance is a pleasure. Do it nicely; do it well. If the invitation was formal enough to be written in the third person, that's the way it should be answered. If it gave you the option of bringing the partner of your choice, say whether you'll be bringing someone and say who it will be.

An acceptance is also the time to clarify anything the invitation didn't make clear. This is especially true when an overnight stay is involved. What precisely does 'Come for the weekend' mean? A good host will have said, 'Come down on Friday evening. The best train back on Sunday is the 4.10.' If the host fails in this, the ball is in your court. The easiest way out is the short blunt route. 'Does that mean I get one of your Sunday lunches? Or will you be booting me out after breakfast?'

LESSON TWO

Having accepted, you may then plan your entrance. By this I mean you may decide **how much punctuality is called for, what you should wear, and whether you should arrive bearing gifts.**

Generally, the more formal the occasion, the stricter the **time-keeping**. An invitation to a grand dinner that calls for your attendance at 7.00 for 7.30, means just that. You can safely arrive at 7.15, but if you arrive at 7.40 everyone will have gone into dinner without you.

On the other hand, if your dear friend Thelma says, 'Come to

dinner on Saturday, 7.30-ish' you can usually interpret that as:
'7.30, Thelma in bathrobe, wretched because she forgot to buy
lemons; 7.45, Maurice in bath with large gin, Thelma filing for
divorce; 8.00, tentative ceasefire, glasses polished, the *miroton
de boeuf* murmuring fragrantly on the Aga, and Thelma chop-
ping parsley. In her bathrobe.' Of course you know Thelma
better than I do. In your case when Thelma says 7.30 she may
mean any time between 7.29 and 7.31. The moral of Lesson Two
is, Know Your Thelmas.

Remove hot food from the scene and you immediately loosen
up the time scale of a party. If you are invited for drinks at six,
my advice to you is to arrive no earlier than 6.30 and no later
than 7.00. Early arrivals drink too much too fast. After all, what
else is there to do when you find yourself alone with a bowl of
punch and Thelma's malevolent cat? Late arrivals suffer a
condition well known to teetotallers – isolation through so-
briety. Everyone is at least two drinks ahead of you. They are
two drinks sillier, louder and happier, and even if you wanted to
you'd never catch up. The party left without you.

What to wear?

Strictly, this shouldn't be your problem. Your host should have
made it clear if there are any special requirements and if there
are not, she should have given you some idea of the general tone
of the occasion.

My grandmother's technique was to keep piling on the neck-
laces and dead foxes until the effect was Definitely Over The
Top, and then add a large pair of marcasite earrings.

My mother took a different line. She has always felt that a nice
jumper and skirt will never let you down.

I have dragged this legacy of sartorial confusion all the way
into middle-age. The best I can tell you is this: as a host I am

always delighted and flattered when someone arrives on my doorstep looking as if they had made an effort, and as a guest, I have felt more awkward and wrong-footed about being too casually dressed than I have ever felt about wearing my best frock.

And **Fancy Dress**? I suppose hosts who mark invitations Fancy Dress Optional get what they deserve. Fancy Dress should never be optional. Party poopers, wallflowers, wet blankets, and anyone else who isn't happy about wearing doublet and hose or strap-on comedy breasts should send their

regrets. Accepters should get themselves round to Berman's Theatrical Costumiers and spare no expense.

And so to the question on everyone's lips. Do we take a bottle?

We should begin at the beginning. How did this bottle thing start? I'll tell you. It started when ordinary British people discovered wine, and at about the same time discovered the pleasure of eating and drinking with friends at home instead of saving up for six months and going to a restaurant. Mainly, they were young people. They fell for the utterly foreign habit of feeding large numbers, cheaply and well on pasta, and of sitting at table, discussing the polemics of R. D. Laing until the wine ran out.

Those were the days, my friends! Being young they were also hard up. It didn't matter. Becky did the *linguine*, Nick supplied the cheese, and everyone brought a bottle. Terrific!

Well, old ways are hard to shake off. Those kitchen table revolutionaries are now in their forties, at least. They have burglar alarms and second homes in the Cévennes. When they ask us to dinner they don't really need or expect that we will contribute. Yet still the land is full of uncertain guests, beset by self-doubt as they hover on the doorstep with a carrier bag from Oddbins.

Back in those days of cheap and cheerful mucking-in, it was perfectly obvious how you intended your bottle to be used. It was to be drunk. Immediately. But if you take a bottle now, what's to be done with it? Your host could open it, but it's likely he has better plans of his own. He could bung it on his wine rack for another time. In which case are you going to feel snubbed? The best way to look at this dilemma is to consider wine as one of many consumable products. Not a measure of your generosity or your sophistication. Just something to swallow. If you presented your host with a jar of homemade marmalade, would you be miffed if he didn't serve it with the smoked mackerel?

We could all safely stop taking bottles. We could declare a moratorium. People have rarely brought me bottles because I am married to Wine.

'Coals to Newcastle!' they cry and give me flowers instead. I'd be happy if they came empty-handed. I really would. But flowers are lovely and so are chocolates. Best of all is my guest who arrives with eggs, still warm from . . . wherever it is that eggs come from.

Of course if ever I'm invited out by struggling young people who don't know where the next meal is coming from, I *shall* take a bottle. A very large bottle indeed.

LESSON THREE

Eat up your greens and don't make a fuss.
Every other person you meet these days seems to have some dietary prohibition or other. Very few of them are issues of life and death. Yet it gets harder to go anywhere and sink your teeth into a coconut-matting canapé without some cheerful chap recounting the symptoms of his coconut-matting related Irritable Colon Syndrome.

Please! Good guests do not do this. Good guests say, 'No chicken for me Joan. The potatoes look absolutely wonderful!' Good guests with grave problems also call up and say 'Joan, I'm on this bitch of a diet. No meat, no wheat, no dairy products. Are you sure you want to be bothered with me?' And if Joan is a good friend as well as a good host she will reply, 'No problem. We'll all eat some of the hundred or so other foods you can manage.'

Good guests work their way around what they don't like. They toy sincerely but inconclusively with items they don't want to eat or drink. And they talk. When a guest is involved in animated conversation with his neighbour no one suspects him of sulking because it's braised liver with kohlrabi.

The finest example of a good guest is HM The Queen. You think you've suffered? You want to tell us about Mavis and the Sweetbreads? Her Majesty could tell you a tale or two. A woman of plain tastes who has been offered more beastly regional dishes than any other member of the human race. She *could* tell you. If she weren't so well-mannered.

Five things never said by good guests

- Are these South African?

- Did you read that *Sunday Times* survey on tapeworms in fish?

- How are Lucy's pet rabbits getting along?

- If I just have three olives and an anchovy I shouldn't exceed my calorie allowance for today.

- . . . so that was on the Tuesday. By the Wednesday I'd blown up like a balloon, terrible griping pains and, about three in the afternoon, I'd just cancelled a squash match and phoned Jen to tell her I was on my way home but the M25 was looking bad, when the diarrhoea started. Very green, very watery, and *very* caustic. A real ring-burner! I'm convinced it was the grey mullet. Anyway, my tongue was terribly coated, and then this thing appeared on my bottom lip. It sort of cracked open and it didn't stop weeping for weeks. Have I seen you since my vasectomy? . . .

And five things never done by good guests

- Bringing uninvited partners, partners of a different name from the one you have been told to expect, or partners of a different gender from that which you've been given to expect.

- Announcing on arrival how pooped, knackered, bilious, intoxicated, cantankerous, morose or suicidal they are feeling.

- Monopolising all available whisky, oxygen and air waves.

- Groping, footsy-ing, knee-nudging and any other under-table hanky-panky unless clearly bidden.

- Outstaying their welcome.

LESSON FOUR

How to say goodbye.

Sometimes there is a real and unavoidable need to leave early. If you know this is going to be the case, you should forewarn your host. Then, provided your host is a well-mannered host, he will allow you to leave without protest.

Sometimes it's only as the occasion unfolds that you realise you're running late. Some hosts say, 'Dinner at 8,' and don't feed you for two hours. Some hosts forget about cross babysitters. In situations like this you must allow your own innate good manners to be compromised by their thoughtlessness. You must state firmly your reasons for leaving, and then go.

Leaving is a skill. If you want to leave and someone else just beat you to making the early getaway, beware of creating a stampede. It is unnerving for a host to have ten people guzzling chocolate marquise one minute and the next to find himself alone with the dishwasher.

Break the news gently. 'Harry, Rita, this has been superb. We've absolutely promised the B S we'll dock by midnight so we must make a move. But we'd love some coffee.'

Then, when your moment comes, act decisively. Say, 'Goodbye and Thank You' and go. There is nothing worse than a departing guest who makes several false exits and starts up fresh conversations each step of the way. Open the door and walk through it. Vamoose! Scram! Depart! Go, damn you!

LESSON FIVE

The next morning write to your host and say thank you.
This may be the last thing under the sun you feel like doing. But maybe cooking you lamb cutlets and hearing about the trouble you've been having with builders was the last thing under the sun Rita and Harry felt like doing. Get out your pen and tell them something nice. One of my all-time favourite guests writes a proper letter within forty-eight hours. In it he recounts at least two things about the evening that he found particularly enjoyable. Another of our guests reviews the evening by postcard, theatre critic style – *I laughed and laughed; wicked! pungent food; a shaky start, a stupendous finish!* These kind and thoughtful friends make it all worthwhile. They compensate for all the silences that could be interpreted so many different ways.

Next time someone entertains you, remember this and after you've reached for the Alka-Seltzer, reach for your writing paper.

HOW TO BE A GOOD SPORT

Don't go to sea in golf shoes or stilettoes. When the skipper shouts 'Lee-oh', duck fast. And never pee over the windward side.

If you have never ridden anything more testing than a donkey, decline your hunting host's offer of a mount. Never feed fudge to a hound. And remember, at 4 in the afternoon those returning from the chase have first call on the hot water.

On the first half of a return drive, best not to pee in your butt. If a bird flies between two guns, the senior gun has priority. In the event of a mishap, you may drop the heaviest of hints, but should not actually say who shot you.

When invited to the races, check which races. For greyhounds wear middle of the road street-wise. For flat racing wear shoes that will hold you up if the going is soft. And for point-to-points wear a thermal vest, three jerseys and a TOG 9 duvet.

Never streak.

Never ask how much longer it's going to go on.

And never, ever, move behind the bowler's arm.

WELL-WORN ADVICE

In olden days a glimpse of stocking was looked on as something shocking. When I was young it was considered risqué to wear a T-shirt without a bra. Nowadays girls wear long-line bras without T-shirts. And so, apparently, anything goes. But does it?

If it is your ambition to turn your back on convention and wear absolutely whatever you please wherever you please, you must either be very old, or very confident, and to be very confident you usually need to be very old. It must be one of the few consolations of old age that you can get away with a feather boa in Sainsbury's.

Some of the currently fashionable ways of dressing are bad manners in themselves. Clothes that reveal too much of something. Usually something female. Before you wear something very short or very low, you should ask yourself this:

'How easy will it be for innocent members of the general public to avoid the sight of my knickers or my breakfast?'

If the answer is 'Only by putting their head inside a paper bag,' you should ask yourself something else:

'Isn't it rather bad manners to deprive them of an easier escape?'

Luckily for the continuation of the human race, most of us know someone who would like to see our knickers. Isn't that enough? Shouldn't the bank teller, and the elderly gentleman sitting opposite you on the bus be left in peace to dream of the knickers of their choice?

I hear several million men muttering, 'Here comes the postfeminist backlash. Just because Laurie Graham shouldn't wear a mini skirt and a lurex bustier she wants all that gorgeous tail to start trudging around in bell-tents!' Not at all. I merely suggest that looking at wobbling flesh, goosepimples, and the top three inches of a bricklayer's bottom should be amongst life's optional extras.

Most people know exactly what they want to wear. By the age of twenty-five they know whether they belong in chain store pastels or something brave from Japan. After that the only times they worry are when they suddenly want to be someone else, or they are invited to something grand.

It's rare for anyone to want to look less properous and sophisticated than they actually are, but not unknown. Dressing down can sometimes be a masterstroke of bad manners. Done with a flourish it can leave everyone else feeling tackily over-dressed. Try it next time you arrive late and discover everyone else is wearing a tux. Say, 'Please! I'd hate anyone to feel awkward! And anyway, you all look jolly nice!' This is not Getting It Right; this is Getting It Wrong – but with panache.

More commonly, wanting to look different is an upward struggle. It can be achieved, but not in my experience, by heading towards the Executive Polyester Suits, priced £39.99. Fashion Editors tell us that if we can't afford Karl Lagerfeld we should buy cotton shirts, cashmere cardigans and woollen trousers. As a matter of fact they're right. Viscose looks like viscose, as I remind myself every time I put it on. Sleeves that are too long or too short make you fidget, and fidgeting saps the confidence. Cheap buttons don't look cheap until you see some that aren't. And exactly the same is true of shoes and belts made of plastic. The advice dished out for years by Nanny and Swiss finishing schools is very boring and very sensible. Dirty shoes, a drooping hemline, or a clutch purse full of old lipsticks and bus

tickets, never helped anyone to feel very fabulous. Buy a clothes brush. Use it.

Buying quality when you can is one thing. Buying quality and wearing it for ever is really one for those who can afford the very best. You need to be seriously rich, and it would be helpful if you lived in the country. Harris tweed and antique leather look best against a backdrop of dog hair and milk churns.

From time to time we all have to go to places where dress is stipulated. This is when you discover whether you are a man, a mouse, or a trouble-maker.

We should begin by distinguishing between private and public occasions. When you accept an invitation you must accept it in all its particulars, or not at all. If you dislike stuffy rules in private houses, you should stop seeing stuffy people.

Black Tie, White Tie, Morning Dress, Red Noses – whatever is stipulated, you must conform to the spirit of the occasion or stay at home and wash your hair.

When you are paying for the privilege of going out, the question of correct dress can be answered another way. You go only where you feel comfortable. As a matter of principle I don't generally take guests to restaurants which insist on jackets and ties. This precludes me and my friends from some excellent grub and occasionally gluttony does get the better of me; but it worries me that those who should be concerned with the quality of food and wine are so distracted by the threat of bomber jacket invasions.

So far as I know there are no longer any restaurants which gib at women in trousers, but there are several which won't admit men in lumberjack shirts. If a man is sufficiently good company I'd be happy to give him lunch even if he turned up in his jockey shorts. This has never happened to date, though I expect it now will. My point is that as long as we behave at table and settle our bill, what we choose to spill our soup down should be our own business. If it can't be, then we should make it our business to patronise other restaurants.

In private then, we should remember our manners, and in public we should choose our own poison. So far so good.

But precisely what does Black Tie mean? Or Smart? Or, pity help us, Smartly Casual?

At the **theatre and opera** you can please yourselves. Many people now do Covent Garden in a sweatshirt just to prove how cool they are about culture. I have to feel sorry for those who love any excuse to dress up. Recently, at a provincial concert hall on a rather special evening, I saw everything from Evening Dress with Fur Stole to Duffle Coat. Somehow the fur stole was the loser. In my excitement about the evening ahead, and my haste to cook dinner for eight and find our mislaid tickets, I ended up in a tracksuit. It was a clean tracksuit, and it was a very cold concert hall. Still it did occur to me later that a little more glitter would have been a good way of showing my anticipation and appreciation of a fine performance.

Black Tie means dinner jacket, matching trousers, white dress shirt and black bow tie for a man, and a visit to a clairvoyant for his partner. No one seems to know for certain any more. Long dresses are worn less and less, so something short but special should be all right, and so usually should evening trousers, but there will be times . . .

I've asked a lot of people's advice about this. The favourite solution is to ask your hostess what she's going to wear. Go on then.

But are you sure you can trust her? Some hostesses are positively mischievous. They say, 'Oh just wear short. Any old short will do.' And then greet you at the door in three thousand pounds worth of Belville Sassoon.

And sometimes there isn't a hostess to ask. Sometimes there's only a host, and a fat lot he cares. Not long ago I was in this situation myself. The invitation said Black Tie. So I asked the man who was to be my partner for the evening.

'Ohhh!' he groaned, 'a frock I should think. Shouldn't you think a frock?'

I said, 'Would I get away with trousers, if they were very special trousers?'

'Trousers?' he said, 'I should think so. Shouldn't you think trousers? Or a frock? As the case may be.'

I have to confess that I saw this sartorial nightmare as an opportunity to be contrary. I broke the rules. I wore the trousers. My partner didn't notice, the doorman turned white,

two Senior Fellows at High Table suffered cardiac arrest, and an ancient college servant told me I looked wonderful. Maybe I'll wear a frock next time. Or maybe I won't.

White Tie means very grand. Outside of royal and diplomatic circles it is rarely called for these days.

With your white tie you wear a tailcoat. You do not wear a woolly waistcoat, or a row of ballpoint pens in your top pocket. For women, white tie is an opportunity to wear a ball gown. But I should tell you this. Some people consider the sight of bare womanly shoulders inappropriate at table. If you are dining with Old Money and White Tie is the order of the day, it is worth remembering to drape a bit of old arras round your décolletage, at least until the roasted meats have been wheeled away.

And while we're on the subject of Old Money, remember these are the people you can trust when you call to enquire about dress:

'We dine in the Chinese Room when we're more than twenty so do *please* wear something warm.'

'Thank you, I'll bear that in mind. And would a long skirt be best, or short?'

'Long, my dear. I usually wear a thing we made out of army blankets in Coronation Year, but Muffin had her last litter on it so I may have to find an alternative. Yes, I think I definitely shall. I simply love new clothes, don't you? I'll probably get Mrs Twiss to run me something up on her Singer. There's sure to be an old servant we could cut up.'

Morning Dress is magic. In Morning Dress even the British Darts Team could look ravishing.

There are many permutations of morning dress, so you can

have whatever you fancy. Black topper. Grey topper with black band. Grey topper with grey band. Black morning coat. Grey morning coat. Single-breasted waistcoat. Double-breasted waistcoat. Plain tie. Spotted tie. You could spend the rest of your natural life in Moss Bros just trying to make up your mind. *Unless* you are a bridegroom.

If you are the bridegroom details like this will already have been decided, and it will only remain for you to stand very still and have your inside leg measured.

'Right Kevin. We've plumped for the dove grey with Edwardian collar and striped tie.'

'Can I not wear my cagoule then?'

'No you cannot. I'm having you looking like Bobby Ewing if it bloody kills me.'

'I'm sure they let me wear my cagoule when I was usher for Donna and Doug. No, I'm wrong. I went straight from work in my boiler suit. What did you say I'd to wear this time?'

Certain other public occasions call for morning dress, like the **Club Enclosure at the Epsom Derby**, and the **Royal Enclosure at Ascot**. But hold on.

You won't get into the Club Enclosure unless you're a member or the guest of a member, and these days they don't seem to let anyone into the Royal Enclosure unless they've been there before. This must mean that as the old buffers with vouchers drop off the perch the Royal Enclosure will get emptier by the year. I wouldn't worry about it myself. You'll have at least as much fun in the Grandstand. However, if you are a woman and you find yourself amongst the fêted and favoured at Epsom or Ascot, you must wear a formal day dress and hat. This is not negotiable.

The place you are most likely to fall foul of rules of dress is the **Royal Regatta at Henley**.

Why anyone would want to watch two boat races every five minutes, followed by wizard boozy japes invented by loud young men in blazers, beats me, but if you think this might be the life for you, listen carefully.

At Henley, absolutely the only place to be is the Steward's Enclosure. If your Uncle Walter is a member, you're as good as in. Otherwise you'll have to find a member to propose you, and another one to second you, and then you'll have to wait about ninety-nine years while your name grinds towards the top of the list and they decide whether you're cut from the right sort of cloth. In the meanwhile you may be interested to know that ladies will not be admitted wearing trousers, denim skirts, culottes, skirts above the knee, or jeans, and men must wear suits, blazer and flannels, and tie or cravat. Henley is possibly the last place on earth you can view quantities of men in cravats.

For **Glyndebourne** I recommend full evening dress, sou'wester and waders.

For **Scottish country dancing** avoid halter-necks and strapless gowns. Why? Put on your halter-neck in the privacy of your own home and ask Cameron to join you in the Gay Gordons. All will be revealed, probably.

Let's talk **Gloves**.

The older you get, the more likely you are to be invited to the kind of banquet where evening gloves are worn. This coincides with the upper part of your arms turning to lightly dimpled junket (if you are lucky) or quivering whalemeat if you are average. Yet another example of what a bitch life can be.

These long gloves can be opened at the wrist and rolled up. Or they can be taken off. Take them off. Rolled back they look unspeakably nasty. Jewels should be worn with gloves as follows: bracelets go *over* them, rings go *under* them. Unless you are using Alexis Carrington Colby Carrington as a role model.

If you are, you'll also need to know how to handle the veiled hat and the fur wrap:

- A **veil** should be raised for the eating of sushi or the lighting of a fag. It may safely be left lowered for sipping champagne and vamping.

- **Furs** always look best on their original owners. So do reptile skins and pieces of ivory. How about some bigger shoulder pads instead?

HOW TO TIE YOUR OWN BOW TIE AND INFLUENCE PEOPLE

First some good news.

Anyone can learn to do it. If you can tie your own shoe laces, you can tie a bow tie. If you can't tie your shoe laces, be sure to look out for my next book – *Auntie Laurie's Guide to Dressing Yourself.*

LESSON ONE

You will require: 1 tie

1 leg – your own will do

Method: Put the fully extended tie under your knee and hold one end in each hand. Close your eyes. Pretend to tie your shoe lace. Open you eyes. What have you done? You've tied a bow, that's what. Agreed, you may not have tied it to a high enough standard for the Garrick Club, and my advice to you would be not to wear it round your knee to the Garrick anyway. But at least you have proved to yourself that you can convert a wilful length of slippery material into something like a bow.

Before you remove it, have a little play with it. By pulling the two loops in opposite directions you can tighten it and adjust it. See! It was skill like this which lit the first caveside barbecue.

HOW NOT TO DO IT . . .

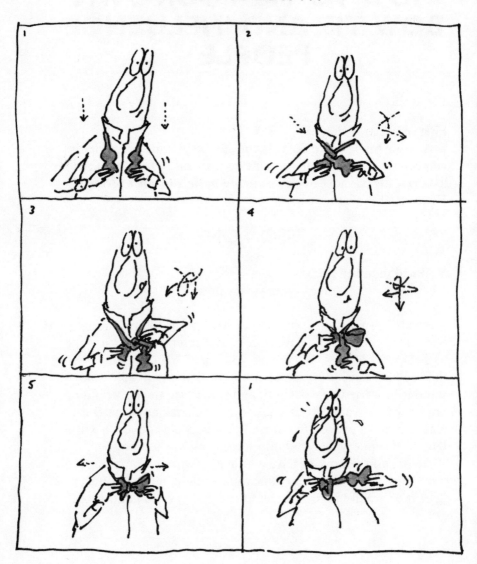

LESSON TWO

You will require: 1 tie
                  1 neck
                  1 mirror

From this moment, when I say Left or Right I mean as seen in the mirror. There is no need to consult a textbook on the Theory of Reflection.

Method: Hang the tie around your neck. Make sure the Left End is about two inches lower than the Right End. Take the Left End and wrap it, over and through the Right End, just as though you were starting a knot.

If you really think about it you will find that what was Left is now Right and vice versa. Never mind. Remember, when I say Left I *still* mean whichever bit is on the left of your reflection.

Left is now shorter than Right.

Take Left and make a loop with it. The closed end of the loop should point left. Hold that loop firmly in position with your left thumb and forefinger. Your thumbs are now of crucial importance. Keep track of them.

Still holding the loop with your left hand, drape the Right End so it hangs straight in front of the loop.

NOW, push this dangly bit up behind the left loop. This is when people start to panic. They call me up and say, 'Laurie, there's nowhere to put it!'

Nonsense. There's a little place you've been keeping ready for this moment. Go back to making a loop. Now drape the Right End straight down. Feel your left thumb. It should feel trapped inside a little tunnel of bow tie. *That's* where you push

79

the dangly bit. Keep poking around until you find it. Then push a loop of tie through it.

You now have two loops. You now have a bow. Congratulations.

LESSON THREE
Undo it and repeat.

PLAIN WORDS FOR BAFFLED GUESTS

'Phone and ask' is the counsel given to guests who aren't sure what to wear. But what if you don't understand the answer?

'It's just supper in the kitchen' translates as:
Very, very casual. Jeans, baggy, friendly old jerseys, *even*, if you absolutely must, the garment that flatters no one over the age of ten, *a tracksuit*.

'Oh, whatever you're happiest in. Truly' translates as:
Suit not necessary for men. Tie optional. Heavenly flat shoes for women, skirts, trousers, whichever you prefer, but do comb your hair.

'We don't dress' means:
Suit and tie. Glamour in the guise of velvet or silk, but not bare flesh.

'We're dressing' means:
We're dressing. Dinner jacket. Black, or not black, as long as it's gorgeous, sparklers, flashes of flesh, and high heels.

FIVE RULES FOR THE
WARDROBE DOOR

if it is your dearest wish never to give offence:

Studied perfection should be ruffled before use.

All attention-seeking items should be donated to Oxfam.

When in doubt, opt for navy.

When in navy, use a clothes brush.

Always check your rearview mirror.

AND FIVE DRESS RULES

for an exciting life:

She who has courage of convictions sometimes dines alone.

He who wears vulgar tie never lacks conversation piece.

When in doubt, pile a bit more on.

Never visit a Colour Consultant.

Don't depend on there being Day-Glo socks in the Hereafter.

ELBOWS ON THE TABLE

Good table manners, at the simplest level, are the many and varied techniques for getting food from plate to digestive system, without breaking the sound barrier, frightening the cat, or forcing those present to wear oilskins and waders. A steady hand is helpful. And the ability to breathe through the nose is important. Manage those and you will find most people very forgiving about pickled onions that go into orbit.

The French, who are right about a great many things at the table, like to see people seated with a nice straight back and their wrists resting gently on the table edge. Teach children to approach all meals from this start position and they will be able to eat anywhere. Next time I have children to rear I'm going to remember that. The English Position, stooped in anticipation of yet another suet pudding is not nearly so elegant. Nor are the hands in the lap. Hands in someone else's lap are for the bedroom.

A napkin seems most useful tucked in at the neck. But, unless you're under three, the correct thing to do is to drape it across your lap. If you lose it, leave it. Fumbling for a lost napkin can bring you into unwelcome contact with other people's ankles.

The number of foods that are complicated to eat or that require an initiation ceremony is very small. The following list will have omissions. Lists always do. And for some, there will be instructions that are surplus to requirements. 'Gracious! Can there really be people who don't know how to eat a crab!'

Never mind. Everyone has a little demon that whispers, 'Do we peel it and see? Or is it part of the table decoration?'

Lists like this always start with Artichokes. This list is different. Here we start with **fishes that look at you**!

Trout

Ignore the way it stares at you. Eat what you can of the side uppermost, picking away at it with your knife and fork. The skin is okay. Eat it if you like skin. You may now have loosened the backbone enough to lift it off the rest of the edible stuff, and in lifting off the backbone you may also lift clear the head and hide it under the watercress garnish. Now you can enjoy the rest of the fish. The only polite way to get rid of a bone in your mouth is to clear it, thoroughly and discreetly of all masticated food, and slip it between your barely parted lips into your fingers and onto the edge of your plate. Do not unload the entire contents of your mouth as though you were a cement mixer.

Whitebait

Again, ignore all those eyes. Just eat them. Heads, skin, all bodily parts. They're a lot cleaner to eat than trout.

Next, fishes that don't stare . . .

A Whole Sole

Start by cutting around the edge. There is a little fringe of bones all the way round and life is simpler without it. Then run your knife right down the middle of the fish, from one end to the other. This will leave you with two hazard-free fillets to enjoy. It's downhill all the way after that. The backbone can be lifted to one side, and you're left with fish. Enjoy!

. . . and fishes that are scarcely dead, we hope:

Oysters

Use a fork to lift the oyster from its half shell, and eat it whole. Drink the juice from the shell, and offer thanks that someone loves you enough to buy you oysters. At a very formal dinner, leave the juice. In France *never* leave the juice.

Mussels

Strictly, you should lift them from their shell with a fork. Leave all the juice till the end, when you may drink it from a spoon. Frenchly, use a half-shell to scoop mussel and juice together, or use a whole empty shell as a pair of pincers, and if any juice remains at the end, mop it up with bread, lick your fingers, and enthuse about the Channel Tunnel.

Prawns

If a prawn is still in its armour you should begin by pulling off its head. Next peel off the shell round its body, and finally pull off the little bit of shell round its tail. Traditionally you should now dibble your fingers in the finger bowl, dry them on your napkin, and eat the little fellow with a knife and fork. If you are dining at Mansion House this is probably the best course of action. Elsewhere, why not take advantage of being up to your elbows in glorious fish, by eating him with your fingers?

Crabs, Lobsters, Crawfish

and anything else that arrives with nutcrackers and long-handled forks: Use everything provided. That crustacean laid down its life that you might eat. The very least you can do is extract every scrap of it from its shell.

Snails

Snails usually come to the table very hot indeed. The tongs are to save your fingers as you gouge each snail out of its shell. In the absence of tongs, or even in the presence of tongs if you are like me and hate unnecessary ironmongery, insulate your fingers with a piece of crusty bread, and use another piece of crusty bread to mop up. This would be frowned on at a State Banquet, but actually you're not very likely to be served dripping, garlicky snails at a State Banquet, are you?

Caviare

Just put a little dollop on a slice of toast, buttered or otherwise, and eat it slowly. You should be so lucky.

Artichokes

The main point of an artichoke is the very small bit which you get to at the end. You need a little pool of sauce for dipping. If the middle of your artichoke has been seen to, the sauce may already be there. Otherwise take some sauce and put it on the side of your plate. Now, start at the outside, pull a leaf off, dip the chubby, whitish end of it in the sauce, and then scrape the bulky part out with your teeth as you hold the thin end between your fingers. Dip, bite, scrape, dip, bite, scrape. Also stack. I should mention stack. You stack the sucked-out leaves on the edge of your plate. The innermost leaves are very thin. Nothing to suck, so don't bother. Then there's a thistly bit. Cut that out, and proceed to the heart of the matter, which you just eat with a knife and fork and wish you could have got there sooner.

Asparagus

English asparagus is a very bad-mannered vegetable. It is limp. Limp, thin and floppy. Asparagus is supposed to be sturdy and erect. You could refuse to eat any other sort as a matter of principle. To eat proper asparagus, pick it up by its paler, fatter end, dip the bud in the sauce, and eat as much of the green end as you can manage. English asparagus will leave you with butter on your chin and a pain in your neck.

Corn Cobs

Cannot be eaten with dignity. Pick it up by its little skewers, or better still, just pick it up. Now gnaw on it, end to end, like a dog with a bone. No need to go to the bathroom afterwards to check your make-up. I can tell you with certainty that your make-up will be looking . . . buttery.

Olives, Cherries, Grapes

and other pippy things: The question is, how do you eject them? And having ejected them, where do you put them? Ejection is simple. Clench your fist. Your thumb and curled forefinger will have made a little hole. Bring your fist to your lips and deposit the stone into this hole. If you are at table you can now transfer it to the edge of your plate. The olive stones you accumulate at peregrinatory drinks parties are trickier. I suggest you either hang around an ashtray until you've had your fill of olives, or take the stones home in your pocket.

Fruit

You should be told that on the grandest of occasions fruit is not eaten with fingers. When in doubt, linger and watch. If a knife and fork are provided, you use them both, to peel the fruit, slice it, and get it into your mouth. No, Brian, not cherries and grapes! Cherries with a knife and fork is definitely a non-starter. Fingers for cherries, but knives and forks for bananas. And oranges? Are you kidding? How about a nice apple?

CHOPSTICKS WITHOUT TEARS

Eating with chopsticks is not difficult, but it takes practice. So does eating with a knife and fork. If you need convincing of that, ask anyone who knew you when you were three years old.

Follow these instructions and practise regularly. But remember, if you let your technique get rusty and you suddenly find yourself dining with *cognoscenti* at The Old Bamboo, better by far to enjoy yourself with a fork and spoon than to struggle with chopsticks and go hungry.

- Chopsticks are tapered. You pick the food up with the narrow end.

- Take a chopstick and rest it in the hollow between your thumb and first finger. Its tapered end should rest between the pad of your ring finger and the tip of your little finger, and be as steady as a rock. This chopstick remains still.

- Hold the other chopstick between your thumb and index finger, balancing it against the base of your index finger and the edge of your middle finger. To move this chopstick you simply move the index and middle fingers.

- To pick up food you use the chopsticks like pincers, keeping the bottom stick still and scissoring with the top stick.

- Buy a bag of stir-fry and practise.

DYING FOR A FAG

A hundred years from now no one will be interested in the etiquette of smoking. As an addiction it has been overtaken by drinking, drugs, money, and television, and there is already something rather quaint about discussing it. Except for this. Those who still smoke do it like men on the run – aggressively. Apologetic smokers are extinct, and anyone you come across nowadays who owns a pack of Silk Cut and a gold-plated Colibri lighter will be full of bluster and defiance.

But first let me show my own colours.

I haven't smoked for fifteen years. Like many women I ditched the habit in the interests of my unborn child. Unlike many reformed smokers I still enjoy the smells and rituals of other people's smoking. That said, I will now state my case. Which is that smoking is a vile, filthy and injurious habit with no place in polite society.

Smoking is unique. By its very nature a smouldering cigarette impinges on everyone else in the room. The cigarette has yet to be invented that burns selectively, curling its smoke tenderly around other smokers and evading bronchitics, asthmatics, small children, and those who prefer to smell of *Giorgio*. Some would say that a squiff of *Giorgio* behind each ear is just as intrusive and inescapable as a burning cigarette and that they are philosophically opposed to being passively perfumed. I might even agree with them. But whatever else you may say about a perfume, so far as we know, none of them damages anyone's health.

Of course the evidence that smoking cigarettes causes disease is terribly flimsy, as any determined smoker will rush to tell you. In fact such evidence as there is has probably been got up, by the Green Party or MI5 or somebody. The likeliest thing is that heart disease and lung cancer are part of a huge Communist propaganda drive. That's it! It's all a plot! And non-smokers are so paranoid they just can't see it!

I don't know about you, but I think smoking *does* damage lungs. Trying to look at it purely from the standpoint of a delicate and wonderful anatomical organ, I'd be very surprised indeed if being kippered thirty times a day was recommended working practice.

Personally I don't need to read any case histories. Instinct tells me that lungs are not built to be barbecued or laid with tarmac. And even if my instincts, and all those statistics are quite wrong, it does nothing to alter the fact that every time you light a fag you make the room stink. Low Tar, Extra-length Menthol, Compressed Camel Dung, makes no difference. Light up and the bottom line is smoke.

Smoke smells. Smokers smell. So do their clothes, hair, breath and fingers. Then there are ashtrays. Also dog-ends, spilled ash and spent matches. And for pipe-smokers you can add pipe-cleaners, and unspeakable gobbets of sludge. Let's face it. Smoking stinks.

With this in mind, **the manners of smoking** become obvious:

- Don't do it in a confined space unless you are very sure no one else there minds.
- If in doubt, ask.
- If someone does object, don't harangue them about the pernicious effects of nail-biting or gum-chewing. Go outside and share your ciggy with the pigeons.

Twenty years ago it was commonplace for cigarettes to be provided at table. Even where they were not invitingly displayed, the correct answer to 'Do you mind if I smoke?' was 'Please, go ahead.' This is no longer necessary.

My **advice to hosts who do mind smoking** is never to be afraid of offending with an objection. Smokers have the thickest skins in the world. Indeed many objectors discover that after agonising, dithering, and finally plucking up the courage to ask people not to smoke, their request is interpreted as an amusing eccentricity that can be ignored. I have a friend who posted NO

SMOKING signs in her kitchen and her car. Everyone who saw them smiled and nodded. They became quite a talking point. Until she tried to enforce them.

As a host, you should feel free to counter rudeness with greater rudeness.

'Donald, you really have the foulest manners of anyone I know. There are five other people at this table trying to enjoy the taste of wild strawberries, and you can't wait even ten minutes for a fag. Another time why don't you give dinner a miss and arrive in time for the port?' Don't worry! Donald won't mind. Not if he's like the Donalds I know.

'Stack me!' he'll say. 'What's eating our lovely hostess this evening? Not getting enough?'

If you smoke before going to table, you should take the signal that food is ready as your cue to stub out your cigarette. And if you've just smoked your last one and it looks like being a long session, avoid bumming smokes from people you hardly know.

In a restaurant with a host who doesn't mind, it's allowable to ask for cigarettes to be ordered and then attempt to pay for them, just the once.

At a banquet the words 'Gentlemen, you may smoke,' now includes the women. You may even be offered a cigar. If you are, and you think you will because it's something you always wanted to try, remember these few things:

- **Cigars** are always bigger than they look.
- Women with cheroot between teeth look very stylish, but smell like Fidel Castro's armpit next morning.
- After six courses of finest British banquetry, washed down with good liquor, a cigar, even a very tiny cigar indeed, is all it takes to turn some people green.

Where you are the guest and the offending smoker is another

guest, or worse, your host, good manners forbid that you say or do anything about it. Smoking is a vile imposition but being an uppity guest is the greater sin.

If you are a smoker, disinclined to quit, or incapable, you will be more kindly received in company if you remember the following rules:

Never in a place or worship, a hospital, in court, in the presence of royalty who are not themselves smoking, or at a formal dinner where a Loyal Toast will be proposed.

Those are absolute prohibitions. To them I would add:

Not between courses, and not in someone else's bedroom – unless you are both agreed that a cigarette is the very thing you need.

ONE FOR THE ROAD

Alcohol is a mind-bender. This is the single most important fact to be remembered by all who drink.

It can transform tense, silent people into delightful companions, and make the dull appear to sparkle. Further down the same bottle, it can lead to loss of reason, judgement, clarity of speech, steadiness of gait and, finally, of consciousness. It makes no difference whether it comes out of a sticky bottle at the back of your kitchen cupboard or a barrel in the cellar of *The Old Sow and Man-Trap*. The chances are it tastes delicious, it is exactly what you most need, and just one swift glass of it is going to make Melvyn Catchpole seem more amusing and desirable.

I'm wholly in favour of it as long as the drinker has no decisions of life and death to make until its effects have worn off. One of the most useful things for a drinker to know is precisely what he's drinking, and how long it's going to have him in its grip.

For the purposes of driving legally, there are some rough but useful rules of thumb worth remembering. The effects of a pint of beer last about two hours. If you drink a bottle of wine over 3 hours, it will take 2 to 3 hours *after* the last drink if you're a man and 3 to 4 hours if you're a woman before you're back to the *legal drinking level*. But it will take 6 hours to be completely metabolised in a man, and 8 or 9 hours in a woman.

I unit	=	I small glass of wine
I bottle of wine	=	approx 8 units
A unit produces blood alcohol concentration of		20mg/100ml in women, 15mg/100ml in men
Alcohol is removed from the blood at the rate of		15mg/100 ml per hour
Legal limit for driving	=	80mg/100ml

Men are generally slower to feel the effects of a drink than women. This is nothing to do with them being slower to *admit* the effects of drink. It's to do with proportions of body fat to body fluid and is yet another well-evidenced example of what a bitch physiology can be. If, like me, you are female, short, and . . . cuddly, your body is likely to concentrate alcohol in the bloodstream so dramatically that a sniff of a cork may be enough to send you sliding under the table. So, if a small chubby woman ever tells you she has a phenomenal head for drink don't believe her. It's the drink talking.

If you want to drink and need to keep your head, there are things you should avoid. **Malt whisky** – because some of them are real whing-dingers and if you haven't had sight of the bottle this could be one of them; **Polish Vodka** – drink it at home on Christmas Eve; and **Schnapps** – best drunk in Amsterdam in the company of someone who knows which hotel you're staying in and is sober enough to find it.

You should also be careful with red wine. Some **Californian, Moroccan and Italian reds** have an alcoholic strength of 16% compared with 12% or less in other wines.

Above all, avoid alcoholic Punch. Don't serve it, don't drink it. I'll tell you why. There is no such thing as a recipe for Punch. You start off honourably enough with two bottles of cheap German and a carton of mango juice. Of course this doesn't smell right at all, so you bung in half a bottle of gin. You put out a few bowls of nutty things, re-apply your deodorant and check your bookshelves to make sure you haven't left *The Hobbit* or *Monty Python's Big Red Book* lying around, and as it's still only half past seven you put in the rest of the gin and a bottle of *Crème de Bananes*. At this stage the situation could still be retrieved. You could pour the whole creation down the drain and nip out for a case of pink Champagne.

But you don't. You discover that you have no musical savvy whatsoever, hide all those David Bowie albums under the bed and change your shirt. You serve yourself a little smackerel of the Punch. It tastes . . . mmm? So you up-end six Club Sodas into it, and the knockings of a bottle of Vermouth.

You are now completely out of control. In Punch-making terms you have shot your bolt. Ideally you should be made to go and lie down in a darkened room. But the chances are you will now enter the manic phase. Bottles of gripe water, miniatures of grenadine, nothing will be safe. Please don't do this, to yourself or your guests.

Drink what you know, sip it slowly and eat. Everyone knows that food, before drinking or with drinks, slows down the absorption of alcohol. Still I go to drinks parties where there is nothing to eat but salted peanuts. Peanuts make you thirsty. Thirst makes you drink deeper and faster. What are people thinking of? Resolve now that one of your contributions to making the world a nicer place will be never to serve drink without food. Your parties will even sound nicer. They will hum and purr, instead of shrieking with flushed throats.

WHAT'S YOURS?

There are **three important things a host should do about drinks:**
- He should decide what drinks he's going to offer and stick to it.
- He should make sure that at least one of the things he's offering is non-alcoholic.
- And he should tell his guests what their options are.

Standing in front of a closed drinks cupboard saying, 'What would you like?' is very bad-mannered and very silly. A thirsty guest doesn't want to play guessing games. If you've only got sherry or sherry, better to say so at once rather than raise false hopes in a gin drinker. And then again, if you've got gin, there's not much point in offering it if you don't also have the things

which go with it. You can make a guest feel a thorough nuisance if you tell him he can have a gin and tonic and then start hissing, 'Did you buy any tonics? Myra I *told* you we needed tonics!'

The simpler you keep the choices, the easier you make things for yourself and your guests. Mixed drinks are a pain in the neck when you're having to be barman, butler, and changer of Rupert's nappy, and your partner hasn't even had the foresight to make extra ice. There are potentially more arguments to be had out of the mixing of six vodka martinis than any other field of human conflict.

Just say, 'Will you have champagne or Tizer?' And make sure

you have enough glasses *before* people arrive. Making a fuss about glasses is very bad manners. There's no need for it. Glasses aren't expensive and you don't need dozens of different shapes. It is not pleasant for a guest to hear hope give way to venom through a closed kitchen door.

'I'm pretty certain Mother's madeira glasses are in the back here somewhere. Angela, will you please keep this step ladder from wobbling! Never mind, we'll have to use the Dartington tumblers instead. What do you mean? In that case perhaps you would like to fetch the remaining Dartington tumbler from the bathroom and explain to Mr and Mrs Lillingstone Lovell that they'll have to have a straw each. This, I have to say, Angela, is typical. Typical!'

When you hear this going on, you feel such a nuisance. You want to say, 'Please! I'll drink it from the bottle!' and then later, when you've had time to think it over, you want to say, 'Why don't you buy some glasses?' And while you're shopping get yourself a corkscrew that you can master. Is there any sight less attractive, any sight more likely to diminish the appetite, than that of man and bottle locked in a futile groin clench while the glasses remain empty?

When you have offered champagne or Tizer be certain that you treat either choice as unremarkable. A guest who asks for Tizer is not quietly hoping that you're going to doctor it with Drambuie. In the United Kingdom there are still many people who don't really believe that. It's because we have a history of standing in pubs till closing time and then going home and washing down our ruined food with a mug of strong tea. Drinking is woven into our imagery of machismo, and as if that isn't bad enough we also have the Temperance Movement. You're a wimp if you don't and a sinner if you do. We need to take a big, brave step away from this.

The moment you stop thinking of *a drink* as your first step to oblivion and start thinking of it as a delicious lubricant and *digestif* you reduce the chances of you or any of your guests falling downstairs.

UPRIGHT GUESTS

When your host says, 'Champagne or Tizer?' you must not reply, 'Campari please.' I know someone who does this. Some people call this artless eccentricity, others think she's making a juvenile bid for attention. Much as I like her for her other qualities, I think she's guilty of bad manners. Of course I could always get some Campari in. In fact I probably would have done by now if she hadn't sulked so monumentally the first time I thwarted her drinking plans.

If your host offers you a drink but doesn't say what, you should assume that you can ask for anything on display. If he meant to hide his Irish whiskey but forgot, that's his hard luck. Years ago there were some people we used to see. After dinner they always offered liqueurs, and I always asked for a Green Chartreuse. I'd never had a Green Chartreuse. To this day I haven't had one. I don't really want one any more. But it took me several dinners to realise that the bottle on their sideboard wasn't for opening. I could have had Benedictine or Cointreau, I could have had a Kummel or some very good Cognac. But the Green Chartreuse was just for looking at. I wonder if it's still there?

At parties where you move around freely there is no excuse for not regulating your own drinking. When you're not actually sipping, keep your glass out of reach of casual topping-up. Try never to be topped up. It makes it impossible to judge how much you've drunk.

At table it should be easier, unless you are in the company of formidable drinkers. There is a fashion now for very large wine glasses. They are a pleasure to drink from, giving you plenty of space to give the wine a good swish round before you taste it, but they will mislead you about quantity.

The glasses in which I serve wine at my table hold *twice* as much as the glasses used for wine in my local. So instead of asking, 'How many glasses have I had?' the important question is, 'How many bottles have we seen off and have I done more than my fair share?'

At formal dinners, where every place setting has a full set of glasses, the correct form is to leave what remains of your wine at the end of a course and move on to the next one. This is a pity. The wine may be finer than anything you could ever hope to buy yourself. You may be abandoning the chance of a lifetime as you hurry on to another, possibly lesser chance of a lifetime. Slow drinkers who find themselves in this situation too often should take courage. **Abandon correct form and give each wine its due.** Unlike smoking between courses, your odd behaviour will affect no one but you, and as a matter of fact everyone else will be getting so tanked up they won't notice.

HOW TO GET THE BETTER OF A WINE LIST

You will fare best if you think of a wine list as a display of what you can have and how much it's going to cost you. It does not contain the secret of instant sophistication, and a confident perusal of it will not guarantee you anything, least of all that Elaine Battersby will allow you to fondle her knee.

Personally, I like short lists. This probably comes of years of living with a man who likes nothing better than an early night with a good wine list.

Begin by deciding what you're going to eat. Marrying the food to the wine instead of the wine to the food is sometimes done, but is really only worth attempting when you are going to drink something exceptional. Try doing it with a bottle of Blue Nun and your companions will rightly think you're a pretentious old fart.

Next, decide roughly how much you want to spend. Deciding *roughly* is always the best idea. It would be a tragedy to miss something wonderful for the sake of coming in on budget.

Champagne

Champagne is heaven. If you had it once at your cousin's wedding and thought it was over-rated, try it again. And again. It is often very good value and is one of the most useful things on a wine list. The promise of champagne will make most guests feel loved and cherished, and whatever you are eating, however widely you've ranged across the menu, you can drink it with everything and you can drink it all the way through a meal.

Avoid half bottles. Unless you know that the restaurant sells a lot of halves the chances are it will be ancient and disappointing. And avoid *brut* champagne unless you are very sure of your own tastes and those of your guests. People who aren't accustomed to champagne seem to enjoy *extra sec* or *sec* a lot more.

Red Wine

The price of the finest of France and of California will bring tears to your eyes. But there is good news. Wine from Chile, Australia, and Italy are very affordable, and likely to be safer ground than something unknown from Spain, which might be superb but has a fighting chance of being filthy.

White Wine

The great white Burgundies will also hurt your pocket. Don't worry if you don't know the name of any great white Burgundies. They will reveal themselves to you by their astronomical price.

But there are plenty of other delicious whites from France, Australia, New Zealand and California. Then there is Germany. Germany produces some exceptional wines. It also produces the sweetish, blended Euro-wines which the British have felt safe with for years. If you're entertaining Aunty Doris, look no further than Liebfraumilch.

Some restaurants list all their white wines together. I can only think they do it as a kind of initiative test. Flunk it and you'll find you've ordered a dessert wine to drink with your fish pie. If the

list doesn't have a dessert wine section and you're tempted to order a white wine you don't know, ask. That's one of the things the smirking *sommelier* is there for.

House Wines
Why not? Very few restaurants take good care of their wines. Why bother ordering something out of the ordinary when you don't know where it's been lying? Château Margaux *is* one of the world's greatest wines, but if a *commis* waiter has been practising his juggling with it, you won't enjoy it at its best. Never be ashamed to order a carafe-wine instead.

The First Taste
When the wine-waiter pours a little of the wine into your glass and stands back, he is giving you the opportunity to see whether there is anything wrong with it. He isn't doing it in case you want to change your mind and order something different.

A wine that smells corky, from having a diseased cork, is actually quite a rarity. A corky wine smells like a musty cupboard in a damp house. The smell is unpleasant and very obvious, and any restaurant will remove the offending bottle fast and replace it. Sometimes a wine smells a bit iffy immediately after it has been opened, but is fine if you give it a minute and swish it round the glass before you try it again.

If you really have some doubts, don't be hurried. When something is wrong with a bottle of wine, time and exposure to the air won't make it go away.

It must also be said that three minutes spent ponderously nosing the Mateus Rosé may impress Aunty Beryl, but if Aunty Beryl has been round the block a few times she's more likely to come to the conclusion that you have developed into a posturing ass. And she wouldn't be wrong.

OUT TO LUNCH

Restaurants used to be used to seduce or to intimidate. Thirty years ago only bohemians or the migratory rich ate in restaurants just because they were hungry. Things have changed. A little. Restaurants are now used for convenience. Also to impress, intimidate, and still, to seduce. We use them with more confidence than previous generations, but our confidence is flawed with anxiety. We often forget what restaurants are about.

A restaurant offers you a table, a chair, food and drink, at a price. It isn't obliged to serve you, no matter how many empty tables it may have, as long as its refusal isn't racist, but if it does agree to serve you it is legally obliged to provide you with a meal and service of reasonable standard and you are obliged to pay for it. That is the deal.

What are we worried about? Briefly, that we will fall over, sit in the wrong place, misunderstand the menu, read the wine list upside down, and fail ever to catch the waiter's eye.

Please try and get this in perspective. Waiters, wine waiters, even maître d's, are not gods. They are ordinary people with fallen arches and clothes which smell of dirty lard. Some of them are good at what they do. Some of them are waiting for that big break at Bristol Old Vic. Don't be frightened by them. Just lead them gently but firmly towards what you require of them. As long as you don't expect the solicitousness of the Savoy at the Greasy Spoon in Inkerman Street, you will be surprised by your own success.

BOOKING

Booking a table obliges you to turn up and the restaurant to provide the table. If you can't make it, even at the very last minute, call and tell them so. In these circumstances the restaurant could make a claim against you for loss of business, but are very unlikely to do so when you've been courteous enough to call them. You never know and they never know when you may need to do substantial business in the future.

Busy restaurants often accept a reservation and then add, 'We'll want your table for another booking by 2.00.' It's up to you. At least they've been frank with you, and if you hate to be chivvied, if you are hoping that lunch may turn into a lost afternoon, you might do better somewhere else.

ARRIVING

This bothers a lot of people. They all want to know the same thing. When host and guest arrive at the restaurant together, who goes first?

This isn't as hard as it looks. If you keep the sort of company where men still hold doors open for women and women sometimes take men out to lunch, it is possible to manage your entrance without confusion. The secret is to take it slowly.

Suppose Gerald has invited Maureen to *Le Vieux Crachoir* and they arrive together. Gerald opens the door. Maureen walks in. Far enough in to let Gerald get in as well, then she stands still.

She doesn't start fannying around with her coat and her umbrella. She just stands still and allows Gerald to overtake her. It's his reservation, so he's in charge.

If Maureen has invited Gerald, life is even simpler. Gerald

holds the door, Maureen steams through and claims her table.

Waiters in the more formal restaurants then make it very clear where Madam is to sit. They do this by pulling out a chair. If you are the guest, take the hint. Accept the offered seat. Allow the waiter to push it back in just before your backside hits it. And when he flourishes your napkin, let him drape it across your lap.

But hear this. A woman accompanied by a man in a restaurant is still widely assumed to be the guest. She may have made the reservation. She may have announced herself clearly. But if she doesn't keep an eagle eye on things the waiter will still slide into the habit of addressing himself to the man.

If you want to be sure that your guest doesn't get presented with the bill, make sure *you* sit in the seat nearest the aisle. Traditionally this is the man's seat. Its occupant picks up the tab. You could probably put a tailor's dummy in that seat and the waiter would bring him the bad news.

ORDERING

A menu used to be a soup-stained card that you fingered nervously in search of Steak and Chips. Nowadays you never know. It may run to several pages. If you are the guest, it may carry no prices. It may be written on a blackboard so distant you need AI eyesight. Worst of all, it may be delivered orally.

'Good evening. I'm Orville and I am your table captain. Your waiters tonight are Peter and Sebastian. We would like to begin by welcoming you to *La Pustule Rouge* and hoping that you will have an enjoyable meal. For *hors d'oeuvres* this evening we have soft-poached gull's eggs on a salad of oak-leaf lettuce dressed with walnut oil, smoked fillet of eel in a Chardonnay-flavoured *coulis de tomates*, or a coarse pâté of ptarmigan breast, prunes and green peppercorns. The *entrées* this evening are sea bass with aubergine mousse, lambs tongues braised in Madeira and served with wild mushrooms, or char-grilled chicken breasts with gooseberry sauce and stir-fried samphire. Any questions?'

'What about Steak and Chips?'

'No. Peter, who is wearing peg-top trousers in a grey slub synthetic and a seersucker shirt in lemon, will now take your orders, while Sebastian struts his stuff in stone-washed denim and a knitted tie.'

The main things to know about menus are these:
- *Table d'hôte* signifies a fixed price meal with a limited choice of alternatives. *A la carte* means if it's on the menu you can have it. Three *hors d'oeuvres*. Three puddings. You are restricted only by your appetite and your purse.
- When in doubt, ask.

Strictly, the host asks the guest what they want to eat and then relays the information to the waiter.

The modern way is for the guest to order direct. **If you are the guest**, take your lead from the host. It is only polite.

If you are the host, lead clearly. Say 'What would you like me to order for you?' or 'Please, go ahead and order if you're ready.' Don't sit picking your nose, dithering over the monkfish. If you guest seems unsure, tell them something you've enjoyed eating there, but don't make it sound like an imperative. Some people take their time because they like reading menus.

When you've decided, order your first two courses. No need to start anticipating the treacle tart. All in good time.

ARE WE DRINKING?

'Are we drinking?' is my least favourite restaurant question bar one. And that one is: 'Are *you* drinking?'

If I say, 'Just a Club Soda for me,' word gets round. 'Laurie's signed the pledge. Don't offer her dinner. That woman is such hard work when she's sober.'

If I say, 'Of course I'm drinking!' they think, 'It's all right for her. That self-employed old lush can sleep it off this afternoon. *I've* got a sales meeting at four.'

As a guest I am happiest when my host says what he wants to do and then asks me if I'll join him. I don't usually mind one way or the other. Being wrong-footed is what I mind.

As a host I like to take an early lead. You get results a lot faster when you say, 'I'm going to drink red wine. Will you join me or would you like to drink something else?' than if you say, 'What'll you have Maureen?'

The Maureens of my acquaintance shilly-shally. They would

be happy with any one of several drinks, and what they are mainly concerned about is not seeming to be too extravagant, or too unworldly. Let Maureen off the hook. And Gerald too. Say, 'I'm going to ask the nice man for a bottle and two glasses. Do you mind?'

AFTERS

Not knowing whether you want dessert is very silly and quite bad-mannered. A host who is running late should have the sense to say, 'I'm so sorry about this. Would you mind if we went straight on to coffee?' If you're offered dessert, assume that the offer is sincere. Don't say, 'I will if you will' And don't ever calorie count. We're not interested.

PAYING

Always check your bill. It used to be considered rude, especially in front of a female guest, but not any more. If there's something wrong and it doesn't look like being resolved quickly, there is an excellent place for a guest to slope off to. The cloakroom. Take a leak, powder your nose. That's what cloakrooms are for. Compacts have returned as fashion accessories and so, it follows, has fixing your face at table. Don't.

The bill is the concern of the person who's paying it. If you're the guest, don't peer at it. If you're the host and you have serious objections to the bill, stay cool. It is generally easier for you to go to the head waiter's desk than it is to have him brought to you.

If the cost of the food and drink is correct but unreasonable because the standard was so bad, or if you feel the service charge hasn't been earned, you can deduct whatever you think fit from the bill and see how the management reacts.

Provided you haven't smashed any chairs or noses there is no point in their sending for a policeman, though they may threaten to, because you're not committing a crime. You are if you walk out without paying at all.

If you pay less than the amount demanded, the restaurant may decide to sue you for the balance of your bill. If you lose heart and pay up under protest, you'll have to sue them to get it back. And you won't, will you?

AND COMPLICATIONS

If your host doesn't show? If you'd like a drink and you've got the price of one, order, drink up, pay for it and go. You might like to leave a message with the head waiter, but if you do, keep it decent.

If there are other people you know in the restaurant? Make do with a smile and a wave if you can. If you can't, proceed as follows. If you are the host, make sure your guest is comfortably seated, make your excuses and pay your friends a flying visit. If you are female and the men at the table you are visiting start to get to their feet, tell them, 'Please don't get up.' Keep things short and sweet. 'How nice to see you! Do let's have lunch soon. May I call you?'

And if you are on the receiving end? Introduce them, very briefly, to whoever you're with. Men stand unless excused. Women remain seated throughout. And hand-shaking is not necessary.

A fly in your soup? If you are paying, complain. If someone else is paying, point it out to them. The correct tone is laconically humorous:

'Gerald, does this place surcharge for insects?'

And soup in your lap? Deal with the practicalities. If you need an ambulance, say so. If you need a change of clothes, say so. If you are the host and in any fit state, ensure that reparation is promised or made immediately. And if you are the scalded guest, go easy with the apologetic laughter. You may be embarrassed but you may also be badly burned. On the other hand, if you're eating in any of the Take-It-Or-Leave-It joints I've been to recently, you'll just be tepidly wet.

A votre santé.

TIPPING

RESTAURANTS

If a service charge is automatically included in the bill, it will say so on the menu and you will be obliged to pay it unless the restaurant has blatantly failed to provide service which is up to standard. Whose standard? Yours.

Where service is not included, add 10 to 15%, according to how satisfied you are. If you're paying by credit card, write *Grats* and the amount you want to tip, and the new total, when you sign the counterfoil. Better still, pay the bill with plastic, and tip the waiter with cash.

CLOAKROOM ATTENDANTS

The size of the coin on the plate does not necessarily indicate the size of the last tip given. More likely it indicates the size of tip fervently hoped for. If you leave your coat, tip when you retrieve it. Just take out your loose change and put some of it on the plate. Even if you have only used the cloakroom for its mirror or its plumbing you will be given the opportunity to show your appreciation. This is entirely a matter for you.

You might want to tip the woman who has sat on a chair listening to you pee, but you might not. After all, you did it all by yourself. Personally, I would only tip for an exceptional lavatorial experience, such as could once be had in Covent Garden

Piazza. Sadly the music, the flowers, the paintings and Reg with the mop have gone for ever.

HAIRDRESSERS

Juniors disappear like mayflies, so tip every visit. Fifty pence is fine but in London more will be appreciated.

Senior stylists are trickier. If your relationship looks like lasting, wait till Christmas and then tip them lavishly. Otherwise you have to manoeuvre yourself into position to drop 20% into his jacket pocket. My hairdresser doesn't wear a jacket. Just very tight trousers. If I tried to slip even 5% into his pocket I could get booked for assault.

Don't tip proprietor-stylists.

TAXI DRIVERS

I throw in 20% like raw meat to a leopard. Sometimes this is accepted with charm and sometimes it is sniffed at like a bad smell. Most people tend to tip cabbies in a hurry and when I'm in a hurry or a flurry I'm likely to overtip. Taxi drivers would deny any such tendency.

HOTELS

Porters depend on tips. No need to shuffle around with a coin sticking to the palm of your hand. If you're shy, you're the only one who is. Fifty pence per bag.

A room-service waiter, valet, night porter or any other member of the hotel staff who performs a one-off service and does it well should be tipped on the spot. A 50p coin or £1, depending on the bearing of the servant and the nature of the service.

Many hotels now add a service charge to the bill as a matter of course. If you've been staying at Fawlty Towers, you shouldn't feel obliged to add more, unless you feel someone has earned a tip for entertainment value. If you have been well cared for, tip your chambermaid, your table waiter and the head waiter. A fiver each. More if you expect to return soon and wish to be gratefully remembered.

If you're a last-minute tipper and you discover that someone you intend to tip is off-duty for the day, leave their tip at Reception in a clearly marked envelope. And next time, don't leave it till the last minute.

AIR TRAVEL

Don't tip anyone except porters. Fifty pence per bag in the UK.
In some countries porters have higher expectations. They will make plain to you how much higher. If you have any sense you'll make sure before you arrive that you know the difference between a reasonable demand and a rip-off.

GRAND HOUSES

If you stay overnight, tip the staff who have looked after you. Leave a £10 note in your room for whoever has unpacked your case, repacked it and tidied up after you.

Butlers are more difficult. They do accept tips, but traditionally only from male guests, and the amount is problematical. The best thing to do is ask your host. If you don't feel you can, a £20 note should do nicely.

Chauffeurs and housekeepers need not be tipped unless they have done you a very big favour indeed.

CLUBS

If it's your club, do what other members do. If it's someone else's club, don't tip.

Finally, when in doubt, tip. You will generally cause less offence by tipping someone who doesn't expect it than you will by not tipping someone who does. Everyone makes mistakes sometimes. These are what make us endearingly human.

SMALL LAPSES

Parents are the starting point for the next generation of door-slammers and phlegm-clearers. They are the guardians of the world's future good manners, better placed than any to make sure that we grow old in a quieter, more gracious place. If only they weren't so incompetent.

First, a little social history.

Children used to be seen but not heard. I'm too young to remember that time myself, but I grew up surrounded by adults who'd been raised that way. Let me tell you what they were like.

They were nice, ordinary people. A little old before their time maybe, but who wouldn't be if they'd spent their golden youth waiting for the *Luftwaffe* to snuff them out? These were people of moderate habits. I can't remember any of them deafening us with 'Two-Way Family Favourites', or dropping their empty Woodbine packets in the street.

My grandmother, uneducated, and grown from uninspiring poor urban stock, was reckoned to be a bit of a tearaway. Actually, the worst she ever did was smoke in the street, and sometimes take a little too much gin in her gin.

These people had been trained from birth to consider others. And this hadn't stunted them. It didn't stop them variously running successful businesses, marrying, procreating, painting in oils, or running off to South America. They were all right. And they did better than just get through life. They wrote letters, mated privately, and raised their hat to ladies in the street.

So what happened? **Worship of the Child.**

It began with the first generation born after the end of the Second World War. By the Sixties the fashion had a hold, and by the Seventies, to deny a child anything, was heresy.

Any little Jack or Beattie coming into the world now will grow up with a strong sense of Self and very little awareness of Others. They will be as objectionable towards their families as they will towards old women in dark alleys, and their parents will blame it on the colouring agent in the orange squash.

My children are different, of course. Anyway, I'm working on it. They have been trained to hold doors open, chew with their mouths closed, and to get to their feet the *instant* a visiting adult enters a room. They think it all utterly pointless. They go into their rooms and mutter sedition. In short, they believe I shall make anachronisms of them all. I do hope so.

Let's begin with birth.

I'm going to assume everyone knows the normal exit plans of a human baby. I wish the newly delivered would make the same assumption at the first ten dinner parties they attend after the birth.

'It really was quite amazing! I mean, one minute Alison was getting terribly strident with suggestions that I move to Tasmania or some other far region of the Solar System. Then she wanted a bedpan. Absolutely convinced she was about to dump in record-breaking quantities. Anyway, knowing what women are like I thought I'd just finish my chapter. Have you read any Bruce Chatwin by the way? Next thing is, there's this thing, this little pickled walnut type of thing bulging horrendously through the perineum. Top of Samson's little head! Ali was looking a mite strained so out came the pinking shears. I told the doc to stitch it back nice and tight. How's the consortium buy-back shaping up, dare one ask?' is not polite table-talk.

You should **get this off you chest privately** with your brother, your father, or the chap in the next office if he seems (a) about to experience something similar himself and (b) eager to listen. Otherwise you should no more discuss it publicly than you would the size of your debts, your insecurities, or your Best Friend.

This applies to the young mother too. Sutures, haemorrhoids, and nipples are strictly for small women-only gatherings, and even then, test the water first. And not-speaking of nipples brings me to **feeding**.

I'm not a life-denying old codger. I swim naked, I dance with abandon . . . well I do on New Year's Eve, and I suckled my babies. You will meet no greater advocate of breast-feeding. I did it with such missionary zeal that there can be few men, resident in South Bedfordshire between 1974 and 1980, who cannot describe in detail the shape and size of my equipment. I never asked, never excused myself. I just whipped one out and did it, right there over the *zabaglione*.

Let me give you some advice. **Don't be a lactating pain in the neck.**

When you are at home you can feed wherever you choose. When you're out, assume that at least one person would prefer you to withdraw. If they're absolutely unanimous that they want you to feed your baby in the midst of them, they'll say so.

Don't take it for granted, even with close family. You may have a granny or a brother-in-law who feels uncomfortable about it.

'Pity him!' you might say. Indeed. It is sad that breasts make so many people sweat. Breasts in newspapers on underground trains make me sweat.

The point of good manners is never knowingly, recklessly or avoidably to make anyone sweat.

One of your friends may have a big problem with breasts. The moment you unleash yours in his sitting room, *his* problem becomes yours. You may be very comfortable. You may know everyone in the room and be absolutely certain they won't mind. Nevertheless get to your feet and say, 'I shall have to feed Samson. Where would be best?'

The likelihood is you'll be shown to a chilly bedroom. Never mind. There is a strange benefit to be had from this. Your baby will concentrate on the matter in hand, and finish dinner a lot faster than he would in the middle of a three-ring circus. This is especially true with babies over the age of four months. They become almost as interested in society as they are in food. When they've allayed the worst pangs of hunger they can't resist swivelling on their little rubber necks to observe, 'Ooh look, there's my Uncle Martin! There's the big yellow mountain called Christine. And there's the great big, ferocious wolf called That Bloody Yorkshire Terrier. Hang about. Someone lit a bonfire on the couch. No. My mistake. Just Grandad and his pipe,' before turning back for another little schnozzle. Up in Martin and Christine's spare room all he'll think is, 'Cold in here. Might as well eat.'

Food inevitably leads to other things. These too should be dealt with privately. **Never change a nappy in company.**

Before someone jumps on me and points out how modern society isolates women with young children and a hundred years ago in some remote backwater of Galicia babies were suckled by the hearth, small children defecated where they stood, and women communed in sisterhood, sharing their last bowl of Pig Bristle Soup, may *I* say that nostalgia is never without its dangers, and that the traditions of nineteenth-century rural Spain don't travel well to Harpenden.

I'm sorry if you feel isolated. I really am. But I don't think scraping the pale khaki residue of Samson's breakfast off Samson's bottom in company is going to make you feel any better. What are you trying to say? That Samson has only passed a small amount of something we're all full of anyway? That your waterproof changing mat is snazzier than anyone else's? Or that you believe childcare is a job to share?

Ah! If that's the case you should address your remarks specifically to your child's other parent. Grand public gestures won't get you nearly as far as low-key persistence. If you have a child whose father thinks his role consists of buying train sets and snarling from an armchair, hand him a soiled Samson and go out for a long, slow walk.

Children grow up. They stop doing it down the leg of their dungarees and do it in a potty instead. But not in front of guests. They learn to walk and talk, but not at everyone else's expense. And eventually they learn to feed themselves. Eventually.

From where I'm looking, modern children are bad news. Being young, they have no natural sense of good manners, and being over-indulged, they will never acquire it. Their parents are confused. They want their children to be free spirits. They want them to taste and smell and feel and vocalise without restriction. Broken conversations, broken furniture. There is no price so high they won't pay it. Because they really believe in the Self Determined Child.

Coincidentally they are also cowards. Being firm with children takes courage. Often you have to be prepared to make an exhibition of yourself in public. As in:

'Put it down or I'll whack you.'

'No.'

Whack.

How much easier to put your own dignity before duty.

'Put it down or I'll whack you.'

'No.'

'Wait till I get you home. And if you won't put it down at least stop twanging it along the fence. Look, that lady's watching you.'

Children who can't be depended upon to obey are nothing but

trouble when you take them out. Parents who allow them to get to that state are guilty of a gross dereliction of good manners.

Finally, there is the lesser offence of **Boring People to Death**. Some mothers can talk of nothing but earache, teething, thread-worms, milk allergies, and earache again. In mixed and lively company this is bad-mannered.

Okay, the world feels small when Samson is three and Phoebe is one and you are hemmed about with pushchairs and babyseats and a Jack-in-the-Box that goes 'Nyaaaah!' I know. I've been there.

But it will stay small if you let it. If you don't keep pushing, the door will never swing open. There must be *something* you can talk about that doesn't involve children or nose drops. And if your partner at dinner gives you a two-hour monologue on bauxite mining, there is no need for you to sink to his depths. Be delightful. Be fanciful. Don't try to head him off at the pass with nappy rash. Remember your manners.

BEASTLY MANNERS

The average family pet is bad manners, lightly disguised with whiskers. This is because it is an animal. Leaving aside all considerations of beauty, obedience and ability to walk on the hind legs, any animal is a liability in polite society.

If you need convincing, take a look at the best of a bad lot. Take a look at **a well-behaved cat**.

Even if you don't like cats, you will concede that they are pretty clean, and they're not inclined to idolatrous worship of the whole human race. They just remember the people who open cans. So much for the good news. Time now for a reminder that well-behaved cats also sharpen their claws, go to the lavatory in next door's vegetable garden, and serenade each other at three in the morning. This is called Being A Cat. It is absolutely the least you will get away with.

Normal cats do many more things than this. Here are a few of them:

- Lean against visitors, pinning them between the cat food cupboard and a hard place.
- Jump on anything with a lap.
- Jump on small furry creatures and bring them to you gift-wrapped but still warm.
- Jump on the table.
- Jump on the table and attempt the art of
  a) inducing loss of appetite by hypnosis *or*
  b) telekinesis of the chicken sandwich.

Because most of these misdemeanours can be committed silently they go unchecked. Are you certain no house-guest of yours has ever had his pillow warmed by a cat's bottom?

Some people are allergic to cats. Some are nervous. Some are *terrified*. If you are a cat-owner you should make it your business to know what your cat is doing and who he's doing it to.

As a guest, never feel obliged to feign a love of cats. It will mean nothing to the cat, who will have seen straight to the truth of the matter. Better, if you're indifferent to them, to cultivate a reputation for bad temper with all animals. This frees you to remove cats from the table or the bed in a loud, ostentatious manner that will be taken seriously.

AND BEASTLIER STILL . . .

You may not be able to take on a dog in this way. He may be bigger than you.

Dog-ownership and good manners are virtually incompatible conditions. If your dog never jumps up, slobbers, bites, scratches, steals, chews, runs away, or barks till you can't hear yourself think, you just about make it. Where did you get a dog like that?

Most dogs are bad news because of the people they live with. Busy, tired, not home much kind of people. People who don't have the time or the charisma to train *anything*. Certainly not a Rottweiler.

A well-mannered dog keeps its paws on the ground. It barks at interlopers until stood down by the Boss and then remains silent. It doesn't beg, steal or even borrow from the table. It sleeps in its basket, comes when called, and only empties its bowels strictly to order. It is an Unnatural Dog. There are about three of these in the whole of the western world.

If you must keep a dog, good manners require you to remember the following points:

- If your guests have to outface the Hound of the Baskervilles every time they want to wash their hands or reach for a buttered scone, they will stop calling.
- If your guests cannot make themselves understood against a motet for Basset Hound and Mongrel, they too will stop calling.
- Dogs stink.
- Wet dogs really stink.
- Mud and dog hair are only fun if you're dressed for them.
- Dogs that copulate with trouser legs are not amusing. Just embarrassing. Dogs that bite are not playful. Just dangerous.

With all this in mind, you must decide. Is your dog beyond correction? And if he is, where are you going to put him to stop him annoying people? In that small room full of wellies and old newspapers? He won't like that.

Hosts may generally assume that guests who prefer their pillows warmed by the back end of an English Setter will say so. Otherwise dogs, back ends, teeth and all, should be kept off guests' beds, personal effects and ankles.

Any dog-owner courageous enough to take his dog into someone else's home should be very sure of his welcome and of his powers of control. Are these people going to be quite relaxed when Tyrone lifts his leg against their Art Deco uplighter? I refuse all doggy visitors without exception. It saves me the embarrassment of having to sue.

Where dogs are involved it's easier to be an affronted guest than an ashamed owner. Emotional distance enables you to deal effectly with Tyrone.

When he cavorts for food, speak to him harshly. It doesn't matter what you actually say. Dogs have a very small vocabulary. The tone of voice is everything with a dog. You might say, 'Tyrone, I should like to see you served, crisply roasted with an orange in your mouth and a watercress garnish,' in a tender, caressing kind of way, and Tyrone will be your friend for life.

But say sharply, 'What a delightful boy!' and he'll slink away to his cushion.

Do the same when he attacks your kneecaps in frenzied greeting, or settles on you as though you were a disgusting old armchair. Be sharp with him. Other guests will admire you. They may even emulate you, in which case the world, or at least the known world of one small dog, will become a nicer place.

And if Tyrone bites? Report him. A dog bite isn't like a glass of undrinkable sherry, tossed in the potted palm, least said soonest mended. A bite is a bite. Get very angry about. Go to the hospital with it. In these circumstances never worry about offending your host. He had it coming.

ABANDONED MANNERS

It is a sad fact that good manners are often left behind at the bedroom door.

Sex is supposed to be chemistry. Good sex is supposed to be mindless spontaneous combustion. Whereas manners are about awareness, of others and of self. **So, aren't good manners and good sex antithetical?** Well yes. And no.

There are two kinds of chemistry in sex. The first occurs across a crowded room. The second occurs later, probably much later and is the kind of chemistry to which the lucky and the wise abandon themselves. In between comes courtship. A time when there is scope for all the good manners you can muster.

THE COME-ON

Sex does take two, so the first thing to ascertain across that crowded room is that you are not misinterpreting the signals. A smile or a wave are not ordinarily used to express serious sexual intent. A wink might be. But a wink might be a friendly expression of sympathetic solidarity. It might just mean, 'I see Connie's pressed you to the Sardine Roulade as well.'

At closer quarters, a laying on of hands may confirm your worst fears. But not necessarily. A touch on the arm is generally free of sexual suggestion. Latins and Americans do it in order to say, 'Hello fellow human being', and Brits do it when you've known them twenty-five years and are absolutely certain not to take it the wrong way.

A hand anywhere else is very different. It calls for an immediate response. Either 'Thank you, but No Thank You,' or 'That's exactly what *I* was thinking. Here's my number.'

Neither response leaves any room for doubt, which makes them very useful, but not necessarily what we want to hear. Disappointment never brings out the best in us. There is no greater test of good manners than The Brush-Off.

THE BRUSH-OFF

Men have a long and appalling history of turning deaf, blind and stupid at this moment in a relationship. Now that women are getting a little practice at it, they are catching them up fast.

Signalling sexual interest in someone takes courage. You have to say, 'I've got a big nose, two GCSEs and sweaty hands. Can I buy you a drink?' and you have to say it loud and clear otherwise it won't be heard. It's a tough thing to do.

Lacking experience of such spiritual vulnerability, women have spent centuries sitting on bar stools taking a pop at the boys.

'What? *You?* Do me a favour, Noddy! I hope I'm never that desperate.'

Isn't that rude? Isn't it the basest, cruellest kind of foul manners, and quite unnecessary? As with all exercises in good manners, put yourself in Noddy's shoes. Doesn't feel very comfortable, does it?

If someone asks you to do something and you don't want to do it, not today, not tomorrow, and not even if he were the last man between here and the end of the motorway, you don't have to have your reply painted along the side of a double-decker bus, you don't need a public address system, and you don't need to call a press conference. You just say 'No.'

If he turns out to be the kind of man who thinks 'No' means 'Maybe', pencil in the press conference.

And if you turn out to be the kind of girl who says 'No' and means 'Maybe', don't be surprised that no one ever believes anything you say.

Yes is a much nicer word to hear than No but we can't always have what we want. Ugly scenes, tantrums and unrequited mooning are all bad manners. Time to move on.

PAYING COURT

Courtship used to involve flowers, chaperones and scented notepaper. It led slowly and deliciously to other things. Or not. Foreplay, which is a praiseworthy pursuit, is not the same thing at all. Before it was invented, foreplay was probably very enjoyable. Now it is a rather self-conscious display of technique.

'All right, Monica, I've indulged you with ten minutes of my amazing manual dexterity. Shall I massage your feet now or get straight on to the ear-nibbling?'

'Colin! Your Mum and Dad'll be here in less than an hour and I've still got the sprouts to do! I told you last time, leave the foreplay and see if there's time for it afterwards.'

This is a shame. Let's bring back courtship. **The rules of courtship** are quaint and frustrating. That's the point of them. They choreograph the early days of a relationship into cautious stages, giving both parties the opportunity to call a halt or unreel a little more line. They recognise the jittery self-loathing that accompanies new love – 'He's so perfect. Why is he being so kind to a girl with lank hair and a bedsit in Acton?' 'What a girl! What a fabulous girl! I wonder why she hasn't noticed my ears?' – and get you through while the abdabs prevail. When you're kept busy holding open doors, and walking on the right side of the footpath you forget about the shape of your ears.

The Rules:
- Make haste slowly.
- Make lavish use of the aphrodisiac effects of genuine attentiveness, consideration and reticence.
- Don't frighten the horses. Or your Uncle Ernie.

GOING PUBLIC

Today there is very little you won't get away with in Hyde Park that fifty years ago demanded a bedroom and lights out. But just because you *can* get away with something doesn't mean you should. There are many things between a man and a woman that are best explored in private. Exotic underwear. Feats of contortion. Demonstrations of little known uses for the tongue. Some outsiders do like to watch this kind of carry on, but they are mainly sad men in raincoats.

I don't want to see Monica and Colin fumbling on the Bakerloo Line and neither do millions of other normal people. Fumbling is not good value for spectators. It is merely embarrassing.

If you are old enough to do it, you are old enough not to do it. Stop it.

AND SO TO BED

Before good manners give way to wild abandon there are a few things that should be cleared up.

First, is this what both of you want? Contrary to popular mythology, men are not on permanent standby for rampant sex.

In addition to rampant, men also get tired, very tired, shy, indifferent, and . . . headaches.

Second, where's it to be? It is not necessarily enough that two consenting adults have consented. How do the rest of your household feel about it? Given that the walls are thin, and the night is young, how about going some place else?

And most important of all, your condom or mine? It is

curiously difficult even at this advanced stage of a relationship to talk rubber goods. If you can't do it in the interests of common-sense, try and do it in the name of good manners. You don't know where she's been. You probably don't want to tell her where you've been. And now there's no need. Because every-one knows condoms are sensible, everyone knows they're ad-vertised on TV and you can buy them absolutely everywhere. And, of course, if everything else is right, using a condom isn't going to spoil anything. To be direct about it removes the burden from your partner. And what could be better manners than that?

... IS THAT IT THEN?

Tooled up? Dressed for the occasion? Good. You are now on your own. If the encounter turns out to be less than ecstatic, it may be due to the weather, it may be due to nervous trading and a falling dollar, or it may be due to the fact that your partner is a lousy lay. It is also conceivable that things will be better next time if you **memorise the following points:**

- Never interrupt sex to take a call from your broker.
- *Match of the Day* is a good alternative to sex but not a good accompaniment.
- Four minutes is perfect for brushing your teeth, boiling an egg, or running a slow mile. But that's about all.
- Filing your nails or reading *Woman's Weekly* are better fitted in before or after.
- 'Ooh ooh ooh, I just remembered what I forgot in Tesco!' is not the animal cry men long to hear.
- Neither is 'Colin! This sheet was clean on today!'

and the following list of turn-offs:

Socks, vests, bedsocks, hairnets, curlers, Vick vapour rub, second-hand beer, crying children, stories of conquests and pleasures past, flatulence, forgetfulness, and worst of all, the wrong name uttered in passion.

GREAT SEX, WRONG FACE

These things happen.

The answer to 'And who is Wendy?' is:

'Wendy? Who said Wendy? Did I say Wendy? I didn't say *Wendy*. I said, "Weh-eh-eh-eh, don't stop!"'

Discoveries made *in flagrante delicto* clearly cannot be denied. People who get caught in someone else's bed usually intended to get caught. They will say they didn't, but there are so many other places for people to play away no one is going to believe them. If you are discovered, withdraw with dignity. Hopping downstairs with one leg in your boxer shorts is not going to retrieve the situation, so you may as well adjust your dress properly before leaving.

If you are the discoverer, you too should withdraw. If your suspicions have just been confirmed, you have wrong-footed those who have betrayed you and there will be time enough for screaming later. And if you didn't have any suspicions? You will be in a state of shock. You may head instinctively to somewhere you can be alone until your head clears. This is a very civilised thing to do.

On the other hand, this is one of those rare situations where you can put fifty pounds' worth of someone else's silk knickers down your waste disposal unit, and emerge with your reputation for good manners unstained.

GREAT DISASTERS

Great disasters call for great panache. When humiliation is on the cards, and flight is impossible, the adrenalin will start to flow. If you're like me, it will take effect just too late to be really useful. My most superb solutions have always come to me half an hour after the event. What follows are all examples of wisdom through hindsight. The thinking behind them is that braving it out is almost always the best thing to do. After all, embarrassment can be a very embarrassing thing.

STATES OF UNDRESS

If you see that another person is undone, assess the scale of the problem. Fortunately for the absent-minded, most of us notice very little about anyone but ourselves. The chances are no one else has noticed and no one else will notice. You should therefore avert your eyes and say nothing.

The only exception I would make is in the event of **a tucked-up skirt**. This arises occasionally when someone has used the lavatory and been over-hasty in rearranging themselves. If you see it, corner the victim swiftly and tell her. It might be you some day.

If you are suddenly aware of being unbuttoned, do yourself up. And if an unfettered breast creeps over the top of your frock, scoop it up proudly and tuck it back in. Some people won't have noticed and at least half of those who did will have enjoyed the sight. *Never* apologise.

Broken knicker elastic is virtually a thing of the past. Knickers these days usually have elasticated stitching that perishes slowly and gives you ample warning. But if you are a slattern, if you ignore the signs, you may suddenly find your knickers round your ankles.

If it happens, you cannot do better than copy Barbara Castle, one of politics' more stylish performers, who lost her drawers in Parliament Street many years ago. What did she do? Think about it. What *could* she do? She stepped out of them, picked them up and dropped them in her bag.

All I can add is this. If you don't have a bag, step out of them, kick them to one side and walk away.

A TOUCH OF THE TITTERS

You are either a titterer or you are not. If you are, learn to recognise when you have reached the point of no return and leave the room immediately. Don't agonise over the disruption you are going to cause by escaping. You will cause more trouble by staying.

If I had practised what I now preach I might never have been asked to leave a meeting of the WI in 1977 or that piano recital in the autumn of 1982. I can't remember what we were laughing about. An innocent word that we foolishly invested with a disgusting new significance, or the shape of someone's ears? It doesn't matter. We knew we were heading for trouble. We could have left with dignity. But we stayed, we sniggered and then left anyway, drummed out, covered in shame.

FAIR COMMENT

Some situations call for compliments to be paid, no matter how insincerely.

If you are asked for your candid opinion, of Tessa's perm or Hugo's recitation, follow the example of Noël Coward, master of the oblique. You may not deliver it as elegantly as he did but his words have stood the test of time. When Hugo asks you breathlessly:

'Well, what did you think?' you must reply:

'Hugo! Words fail me!'

WORLD WAR THREE

A fight is a frightening thing to deal with, but if you don't it will escalate. They always do. If it's your party, it's your fight. Calm women, and jugs of cold water are good to have as back-ups. A sober fight is the worst, but you are at least likely to have some warning of it. Sober fights are often the culmination of hours of needling. Prevention is better than cure. Tell them both to leave.

Drunken fights are something else. They may lead to bloodshed, but fighting drunks are just as likely to end up asleep or vowing their undying allegiance to each other. Bring on the calm women and the jugs of cold water. And take no prisoners.

ONE LUMP OR TWENTY

At **formal dinners** the fish and meat dishes often arrive sliced for service and then reconstituted for visual impact. The waiter appears at your left shoulder with a plate of sliced pork and

invites you to serve yourself. He clearly intends you to take one slice. You intend to take one slice. But somehow the slice you choose doesn't want to be separated from the others. Before you can say, 'Blunt knife,' you have half a pig on your plate.

The correct procedure is as follows:

Say to the waiter, 'One moment.'

Cut free what you want to keep. Transfer everything else back to the serving dish. And add loudly, 'Please make sure the other slices are properly cut before you offer them.'

Don't apologise. And don't mop splashes of gravy off those sitting nearest to you, even if you know them very intimately indeed.

STAINED REPUTATIONS

Blood stains on someone else's sheets and mattress are a delicate matter. Clearly you didn't want it to happen and will be feeling mortified that it has. An apology will be as awkward to receive as it will be to offer. Don't bother. Roughly half the population of the world menstruates for forty years of its life, it isn't a lot of fun, and the likelihood is that the person who is going to launder the sheets will think no more of it than she will of all the other personal detritus left for her to deal with on a typical Monday morning.

Say nothing. Send her some flowers.

Red wine tipped on the tablecloth, **black coffee** spilled on the Chinese rug, being dramatically public, mishaps like this need handling differently.

An apology is natural and appropriate. Having apologised you should then follow the wishes of your host. If she wants to do the business with fistfuls of salt and buckets of cold water, do what you can to help. This will probably mean staying out of her way. If she doesn't want to deal with it immediately, respect her wishes. It may be her way of being gracious.

If it looks really bad, if you think you may have ruined something very special, ask discreetly and privately if you can do something to compensate. The answer is likely to be No. Send flowers instead. **Send flowers anyway.**

AND WORSE MESSES STILL . . .

If you are going to be sick, move heaven and earth to do it privately. Interrupt Act III. Offend nobility. Knock over women and children. Just get out of the room.

If you are merely a bystander, feign illness and run. The world is full of people who are never happier than when coping with a crisis. Medical emergencies bring out the best in them. Show them a pavement pizza, give them a mop and a bottle of disinfectant and they become the life and soul of the party. Let them.

Life is full of cruel surprises. The crushing snub, the unzipped fly. You could cringe. You could go home and bite your pillow. You could die of shame right there, on the spot. Don't do that. It's such bad manners.

INDEX